1%WARRIOR™
LEADERSHIP

A.J. Madden

Dedication:

A thread that runs through my whole life is exposure to great leadership, starting at a young age. My biggest leadership influences are my parents. They live a life of integrity, strength, and service to their families and communities. I am beyond fortunate to call them Dad and Mom, and I dedicate this book to them.

Table of Contents

Introduction

Leadership is the answer.

What is the question?

It doesn't matter.

Every problem is a leadership problem.

Every solution is a leadership solution.

Any organizational problem can be solved by better leadership.

And it starts with how we lead ourselves. The person in the mirror.

To understand the 1% Warrior Leader philosophy, you must first understand the Japanese principle of "Kaizen".

Kaizen is a Japanese philosophy of consistent, incremental progress.

Masaaki Imai, a Japanese management consultant with over 50 years of experience, is known for his work on Kaizen. Kaizen, in his words:

"The Kaizen Philosophy assumes that our way of life—be it our working life, our social life, or our home life - deserves to be constantly improved."

The message of the Kaizen strategy is that not a day should go by without some kind of improvement being made somewhere in the company.

Kaizen means ongoing improvement involving everybody, without spending much money.

You can't do kaizen just once or twice and expect immediate results. You have to be in it for the long haul."

My definition of a 1% Warrior Leader:

"A leader who gets 1% better every day in the service of something greater. The best way to become a top 1% leader is to simply get 1% better each day until you get there."

When a 1% Warrior Leader harnesses the magic of "compound interest" and focuses on getting "1% better than yesterday", tremendous improvements and transformations can occur in a short period of time.

When you simply get 1% better each day, through time and the compounded results, this is what occurs over the following increments:

41 days = 50% improvement

70 days = 200% improvement

90 days = 244% improvement

181 days = 600% improvement

232 days = 1000% improvement

365 days = 3700% improvement

In 70 days (ten weeks), you can double your current success.

In 232 days or roughly seven and a half months, you can increase it by ten times.

Billionaire investor, Charlie Munger, calls compound interest "the 8th wonder of the world".

The power of getting 1% better each day cannot be overstated. You're reading this book because you want to be a better leader. What you'll receive within are the "best of the best" principles and practices I've learned from two decades in the arena. This book encompasses the lessons learned through my 40,000 hours plus of study, practice, and teaching the mindsets and habits of high-performance leadership.

What you'll learn:

The 12 Power Principles of a 1% Warrior Leader

The Leadership System That Never Fails: The three simple steps to "Win the Day" as a leader

The 21 Powerful Questions asked by the most effective leaders

The Seven Most Common Challenges That Break (Or Make) Leaders, and the Seventeen Key Solutions

The Seven Tests of The Best that only the strongest leaders pass

The awesomely effective 1% Warrior Goal Mastery System

The Beat the Clock Time Mastery System designed to give you hundreds of hours back a year

The Talent Mastery best recruiting and hiring practices

The Culture Mastery System: How to create and sustain an A++ organizational culture

Your 1% Warrior Leadership book will deliver you 81 leadership tools and nine "leadership systems". You will learn to be a success scientist and excellence engineer for your team and organization. The best leaders think like scientists and engineers.

Effective leaders "test and experiment" like scientists to *discover what the best practices are for the success and happiness of the organization and its people*. After testing and experimenting, they double down on what works and discard what doesn't. An effective scientist conducts research to advance knowledge in a specific area. An effective leader conducts research by listening to his or her people in order to advance the team's happiness and growth.

The best leaders also think like engineers. The word engineer comes from the Latin word *ingeniare*, which means "to create, design, devise". An engineer designs, builds, or maintains machines or structures. Engineers create and analyze complex systems. An organization of people is a complex system. Our role as a leader is to help *create and maintain the systems that perpetuate the success and happiness of our people*.

1% Warrior Leadership is a handbook of simple and effective systems for leaders who have anywhere from "one to one billion followers". It works if you do the work.

Success leaves clues. This book contains "best practices" from the playbooks of many of the greatest leaders on the planet, as well as my own personal experience in the trenches. All simplified into effective *leadership systems* designed to help you and your people win.

Don't overthink this. It's not that complicated.

It doesn't matter what the question is.

Leadership is the answer.

1. The 12 Power Principles of 1% Warrior Leadership

> *"Leading by example isn't the best way to lead.
> It's the only way to lead."*
>
> *-Vince Lombardi*

A "1% Warrior Leader" strives to be useful to their family, organization, and community.

The following twelve "best practices" were assembled through a combination of:

1. Studying those who are widely regarded as some of the most effective and respected leaders in modern history

2. My own personal "in the trenches" leadership experience over the last 20 years

There are 12 Power Principles of a 1% Warrior Leader:

1. Live by Example

2. Heroic Mission (Future Positive)

3. Ferocious Simplicity

4. Focus, Certainty, and Enthusiasm (Useful Charisma)

5. Energizer

6. Learn, Learn, Learn (Deep Domain Expertise)

7. Over-Communicator (Simplicity, Repetition, and Conviction)

8. High Warmth (Know, Care, and Believe in)

9. High Standards

10. Success is in the Setup

11. Listen, Shoot, Believe

12. Win

These principles can be applied to leadership in all disciplines:

Business management

Sports coaching

Parenting

Public service

And anyone in a position of leadership, anywhere, any time, any place.

> *"Do everything you ask of those you command."*
> *-General George S. Patton*

The 12 Power Principles

1. 1% Warrior Leaders Live by Example.

"Living by Example" is a step above and beyond "leading by example".

It means living your life in a way, all day long, that inspires others.

Living by example also includes what you DON'T do.

Very important: if you are participating in mindless negativity, STOP.

Gossiping, condemning, complaining, blaming, and venting.

This is easily one of the worst things you can do as a leader. You will lose respect each and every time you are mindlessly negative.

In his brilliant book, "59 Seconds", Dr. Richard Wiseman discusses this transference:

"When you gossip about another person, listeners unconsciously associate you with the characteristics you are describing, ultimately leading to those characteristics being 'transferred' to you."

Not only does mindless negativity set a terrible example for your team, but the characteristics in others you are gossiping about will be transferred to you.

Leaders are always under the microscope. Everything you say and do is under scrutiny at all times. Accept this like you chose it.

Act accordingly.

Speak accordingly.

Live accordingly.

> *"The most important thing is to try and inspire people so that they can be great in whatever they want to do."*
> *-Kobe Bryant*

2. 1% Warrior Leaders make each day a "Heroic Mission", focused on creating a positive future. They focus on the Future (a Better Today and Tomorrow) and the Positive (Growth and Gratitude) far more than they focus on the past and the negative.

1. Failing organizations and leaders focus on the past far more than they do the present and the future. 1% Warrior Leaders push their teams to figure out what they can do to make today better than yesterday, and tomorrow better than today.

2. Failing organizations and leaders focus on what is going wrong (problems) and mindless negativity (gossiping, condemning, complaining, blaming, and venting) far more than they do on solutions and what is going right. 1% Warrior Leaders push their teams towards Growth and Gratitude.

Advice that Steve Jobs gave to Salesforce founder, Marc Benioff:

"If you want to be a great CEO, be mindful and project the future."

3. 1% Warrior Leaders operate with Ferocious Simplicity.

Apple founder, Steve Jobs, was fanatical about keeping a narrow focus.

Mozart believed that "True genius resides in simplicity".

Albert Einstein thought the highest level of genius was "Simple".

It is very easy to drown in opportunities and ideas.

You must say "No" to the good, so you can say "Yes" to the outstanding.

1% Warrior Leaders focus on the vital few most important things, and say "no" to almost everything else.

> *"Stop doing everything that doesn't contribute to you being number one."*
> *-Seth Godin, The Dip*

4. 1% Warrior Leaders bring three types of "Charismatic Energies": Focus, Certainty, and Enthusiasm.

Focus, Certainty, and Enthusiasm are highly contagious to everyone around us.

1. 1% Warrior Leaders bring Focus to the individual in front of them, without distraction, interruption, or judgment. 1% Warrior Leaders are Expert Listeners; they listen deeply and consistently to their team members, customers, family, and community.

"Plug that hole—that one, right in the middle of your face—that drains you of your vital life force. Watch what happens. Watch how much better you get."

-Ryan Holiday

2. 1% Warrior Leaders are Certain in themselves, Certain in their people, Certain in their mission, and Certain in their organization.

"When Bear Bryant walked out on the football field, self-confidence hung in the air around him like a fine mist. That was good for at least one touchdown for Alabama. Confidence was a secret ingredient of Bryant's success and Vince Lombardi's legend."

-Joe Paterno

3. 1% Warrior Leaders show Enthusiasm in everything they do. They show Enthusiasm that tomorrow will be better than today. Supreme optimism.

"People respond to energy much more than they do words. They respond to what they feel, not what they hear and see (hear and see are low-level influencers). Energy, spirit, transfer of energy is what people respond to. The best leaders come from a place of monster conviction and belief."

-Ed Mylett

5. 1% Warrior Leaders are Energizers.

As a leader, when you walk in the room, the positive energy either goes up or down.

The emotional temperature either goes up or down.

You either give energy, or you take it away.

There is no neutral.

One of the true tests of a leader is this: Can you energize others on the days you don't feel like it?

If you can, that is a mark of a true professional.

In order to energize others, you must maximize your energy first.

Eat for energy, move every day, and prioritize quality sleep.

> "If a boss can't energize and excite and make people want to be there, he or she shouldn't have that title."
>
> -Jack Welch

6. 1% Warrior Leaders Learn, Learn, Learn.

1% Warrior Leaders strive for Deep Domain Expertise.

Leaders are readers.

Leaders are learners.

Knowledge is the simplest, least expensive competitive advantage you can have.

Outlearn the competition.

Never stop listening and learning.

> "Leadership and learning are indispensable to each other."
>
> -John F. Kennedy

7. 1% Warrior Leaders Over-Communicate with Simplicity, Repetition, and Conviction.

1% Warrior Leaders use Simplicity, Repetition, and Conviction to positively persuade others to do things that benefit the individual, their family, or their organization. Positive results include better health, less stress, more happiness, more career and financial success, or better relationships for everyone involved.

1. Simplicity = a few simple messages or mantras.

"Simple ideas stick, complicated ones don't."

-Chip Heath

2. Repetition = repeated over and over again, over-communicated; when someone gets tired of hearing something, that's when it begins to sink in.

"The Rule of 7 is a marketing principle that states that your prospects need to come across your offer at least seven times before they really notice it and start to take action."

-John Stevens

3. Conviction = 100% commitment to and belief in the message.

"It's not what you say or do that counts, but what your posture is when you say or do it."

-Robert J. Ringer

8. 1% Warrior Leaders create High Warmth because they Know, Care, and Believe in their people.

1. They KNOW what makes each individual team member happy, sad, where they've been, and where they want to go.

2. They CARE about people's success and happiness.

3. They BELIEVE IN people, sometimes more than that person believes in themselves.

Believing in your people has a powerful psychological effect on their performance.

Decades of research in psychology has provided strong evidence that the high expectations from others lead to improved personal performance.

Dr. Robert Rosenthal defined the "Pygmalion Effect" as "the phenomenon whereby one person's expectation for another person's behavior comes to serve as a self-fulfilling prophecy."

Rosenthal also studied how powerful non-verbal communication was in the Pygmalion Effect. The majority of human expression is made up of the non-verbal communication of vocal tonality, facial expressions, gestures, and posture.

As a leader, increasing your expectation of the follower's performance will result in better performance by the follower.

> "Doctors have great power to give people greater confidence in their ability to heal themselves. I've had many patients over the years who said that the most important thing I did for them was that I was the only doctor who told them they could get better. Astonishing."
>
> -Dr. Andrew Weil

9. 1% Warrior Leaders have High Standards for everyone in their life and organization, starting most importantly with themselves. The person in the mirror.

> "If you take care of the little things,
> the big things will take care of themselves."
>
> -Joe Paterno

1. They know details are crucial because all the little things add up to the big picture. When you take care of the little things, the big things take care of themselves.

2. They are able to challenge people to live up to standards, without robbing that person of their dignity or motivation.

3. The secret to standards: the vast majority of people will rise to high standards when they are simple, clearly stated, over-communicated, and when someone believes that they are capable of achieving them.

> "Never walk by a mistake
> or you just set a new lower standard."
>
> -Ann Dunwoody, U.S. Army 4-Star General

1% Warrior Leaders keep the following "Three Agreements":

1. They show up on time for the commitments they make.

2. They do what they say they're going to do. They keep their word. They don't cancel commitments the day of or at the last minute.

3. They are completely focused on the person they are talking to. They are fully present in the conversation without distractions such as smartphones, the television, conversations with other people, etc.

What does keeping these Three Agreements show to others? That we respect them, we care about them, and that they are important to us.

Additionally, keeping the Three Agreements gives us the "high ground" in every interaction, commanding the respect and attention we need to be effective leaders.

> *"A person who cannot keep appointments on time, cannot keep scheduled commitments, or cannot stick to a schedule cannot be trusted in other ways either."*
>
> *-Dan Kennedy*

10. 1% Warrior Leaders know that "Success is in the Setup".

1% Warrior Leaders create an environment that attracts the best talent in their field like a magnet.

The best talent in any field has three simple yet crucial qualities:

1. Energy. They have a passion for and are energized by the work of the trade. And they also have the ability to energize their teammates.

2. High Standards. They have high personal standards inside and outside of work. They do what they say they were going to do, plus a little extra. They take pride in everything they do. They are self-motivated.

3. High Warmth. 1% Warrior Leaders hire the smile. People with high warmth treat others well. They are lifters, not leaners.

> *"Bill Gates has said that if you took the twenty smartest people out of Microsoft it would be an insignificant company, and if you ask around the company what its core competency is, they don't say anything about software. They say it's hiring."*
>
> *-Geoff Colvin*

11. 1% Warrior Leaders are Expert Listeners, Straight Shooters, and True Believers

1. They Listen Expertly to the person in front of them. Without distraction. Without judgement. Without feeling the need to interrupt or interject their opinion every 30 seconds.

"The answer to your customer, to your spouse or kid: they already know the answer. There is greatness already in us, we just have to pull it out."

-Daniel Burrus

2. They Shoot Straight with people and are honest about ways that person can improve, ways that person is letting people down, serious mistakes that person is making, etc. They do this in a way that lets people keep their dignity. And they do it because they care deeply about the person. They always let people know where they stand, good or bad.

"To love someone is to tell them the truth even if you are going to suffer for it."

-Patrick Lencioni

3. They Believe Deeply in others. They see people as the best version of themselves. They see people as they could be, not as they are.

> "People are starving for encouragement
> and they don't need much."

-Dr. Jordan Peterson

12. 1% Warrior Leaders know how to Win.

Whatever their definition of winning is.

Whatever their most important metric is. Examples:

Being the "best place to work" and winning an award for that.

Hitting a company sales goal for the year.

Keeping the business alive through a serious crisis.

Visiting every single store in the company each month.

Having one sincere conversation with every single employee at least once every six months.

Not missing a single game of their child's sports season.

Here's the real secret to winning: not focusing on winning.

But instead, focusing on the daily process of doing the very few most important things. Consistently over time. With very few misses or interruptions.

> *"The difference between a true leader and a pretend leader is they can, even on those days that they don't feel like it, transcend their personal feelings and still be a cheerleader, coach, and mentor."*
>
> *-Dan Peña*

Summary:

There are 12 Power Principles of a 1% Warrior Leader:

1. Live by Example

2. Heroic Mission (Future Positive)

3. Ferocious Simplicity

4. Focus, Certainty, and Enthusiasm (Useful Charisma)

5. Energizer

6. Learn, Learn, Learn (Deep Domain Expertise)

7. Over-Communicator (Simplicity, Repetition, and Conviction)

8. High Warmth (Know, Care, and Believe in)

9. High Standards

10. Success is in the Setup

11. Listen, Shoot, Believe

12. Win

Rate yourself on a 1-10 scale, 10 being best, in each of the twelve principles.

Pick the one or two principles that you gave yourself the lowest scores in, and focus on improving your abilities there for the next 30 to 90 days.

Yourself, and everyone around you, will benefit greatly.

> *"The best way to predict your future is to create it."*
>
> *-Abraham Lincoln*

2. Win the Day: The Leadership System That Never Fails

The following is what I call it "Leadership System That Never Fails". It is the most simple, efficient, and powerful process I have found to improve leadership ability.

It can be applied to every type of leadership imagined, from parenting to business, to military commanders.

The Three Steps to Win the Day

The following are the three daily habits that make up the Leadership System That Never Fails:

1. ENERGIZE and prioritize your #1 Performance Enhancer.

2. Have ONE Three-Minute Magic Conversation.

3. UPGRADE Your Expertise for 15 minutes.

Ask yourself at the end of the day if you did these three simple things.

If you did, it was a good day.

Step One: Energize

> *"The only way you can light other people on fire is to be lit yourself on the inside."*
>
> *-Tim Grover, strength and conditioning coach of Michael Jordan and Kobe Bryant*

Maximize your energy first so you can energize others.

> *"Your health always comes first, because it drives your performance at everything else. Your friends and family come second, and work is a close third. Most people live according to the exact opposite order: work first, family and relationships second, and themselves dead last. The fact is, you will never be the worker, partner, parent or friend that you want to be if you don't prioritize your own health and happiness."*
>
> *-Dave Asprey*

Know your #1 Performance Enhancer.

To figure out exactly what it is, ask yourself this simple question:

What is the one thing, that if I don't do it, my day is not good?

Is it eating, moving, or sleeping?

When you don't do this ONE thing, you may feel:

Cranky

Irritable

Brain fog

And you don't make your best decisions.

Whatever your #1 Performance Enhancer is, prioritize it every day. If you miss one day, it's not the end of the world. Just don't miss TWO days in a row. Progress over perfection.

> "The most important thing in life is your energy. Without energy, you can't do anything!"
>
> -Tony Robbins

If your #1 Performance Enhancer is eating, here are some examples of things you can prioritize:

Eating foods that give you energy and avoiding foods that drain your energy.

Eating every three hours.

Fasting for 16 hours a day.

Eating a good breakfast.

Reducing or eliminating the sugars and processed carbohydrates in your diet.

> "Let go of foods that don't serve you. Become more aware and be conscious of your body. After you eat a meal, you should feel very energized and have a ton of energy. If you don't, that means the food might be holding you down."
>
> -Aaron Doughty

If your #1 Performance Enhancer is <u>movement</u>:

Do what moves you. Find a type of exercise that you enjoy doing with people you enjoy doing it with. Examples: biking, swimming, basketball, soccer, yoga, resistance training, Brazilian Jiu-Jitsu, kickboxing, walking, hiking, running, etc.

If movement maximizes your energy:

Prioritize 30 minutes of exercise before or after work

And/or

Go for a 30-minute walk during lunch.

If your #1 Performance Enhancer is <u>sleep</u>:

Prioritize 8 hours of quality sleep and guard that time religiously.

In a landmark study of elite performers by K. Ander's Ericsson, the best of the elite performers slept for 8 hours and 36 minutes on average; the average American gets just 6 hours and 36 minutes per night on weeknights.

Ways to maximize your quality sleep:

Go to bed and wake up at the same time every day

Stop consuming caffeine at least eight hours before bedtime

Practice good sleep hygiene: eliminate all light, eliminate electronics, keep the room temperature around 66 degrees, and invest in a good mattress

Set a "reverse alarm" to remind you when to go to sleep

> *"Diet, exercise, and work ethic don't hold a candle to how sleep can revolutionize the way you live, love, parent, and lead."*
>
> *-Dr. Brené Brown*

Tom Brady goes to bed at 8:30 p.m.

Mark Wahlberg goes to bed at 7:30 p.m.

Jeff Bezos gets 8 hours of sleep per night.

Michael Phelps slept eight hours a night and then took a two to three-hour nap every afternoon.

Sleep is the number one Performance Enhancer for most people. Quality sleep gives you the energy to exercise, the willpower to stick to a nutrition plan, improves your mood, and can increase your happiness.

If your sleep is already of good quality and duration, work on your nutrition or exercise.

Whichever one is most important to you having a high energy day.

A few additional simple tips to upgrade your energy:

Every morning, write down three things you're grateful for from the last 24 hours.

Clean and organize your environment.

Drink 16 ounces of water when you wake up before you do anything else. Aim to drink at least half of your body weight in ounces of water each day. Example: a 150-pound person would drink 75 ounces of water per day.

Spend more time with people who energize you, and less time with people that drain your energy.

> *"If you can do something for 30 days,*
> *you can do it forever."*
>
> *-Rachel Hollis*

Go on a "30-day no social media, no news, or no negativity diet". Cut out scrolling through social media feeds. Cut out reading, watching, or listening to negative news. Or cut out making any negative statements.

The "30-day No Negativity Challenge": For 30 days, no complaining, gossiping, blaming, venting, or condemning others. If you do, you have 10 seconds to change your words into something positive.

Step 2: The Three-Minute Magic Conversation

> *"Love and accountability are the two main*
> *ingredients of leadership."*
>
> *Jon Gordon*

Have one Three-Minute Magic Conversation daily. This is what it looks like in three simple steps:

Part One: Catch

Catch the person doing something right (reinforcement of the positive). Give a sincere and specific compliment.

Catching people doing things right is the most important step of the three. If you could ONLY do one of the three steps daily, make it this one.

> *"There are no rules without relationships."*
> *-Mack Brown*

Part Two: Challenge

Ask the person "what is the biggest challenge you are facing right now, and can I do anything to help?"

OR

Challenge them directly to improve something in a way that inspires them to do better

> *"A team of Stanford, Yale, and Columbia researchers discovered that one particular form of feedback boosted student effort on their written essays so immensely that they deemed it "magical feedback". It consisted of one simple phrase: I'm giving you these comments because I have very high expectations and I know that you can reach them. When you look more closely at the sentence, it contains three separate cues:*
> *1. You are part of this group.*
> *2. This group is special; we have high standards here.*
> *3. I believe you can reach those standards.*
> *These signals provide a clear message that lights up the unconscious brain: Here is a safe place to give effort."*
> *-Daniel Coyle, The Culture Code*

Part Three: Cross-Examine

Learn something new about the person. This will fall into the following four categories:

What makes them happy?

What makes them sad?

Where have they been?

Where do they want to go?

Ask them, "What do you think?" This could be about anything.

> *"You can be unbelievably demanding and challenging on people if they know how much you care."*
>
> *-James Franklin*

Have this simple conversation EVERY DAY with just ONE PERSON.

You can have these conversations in as little as three minutes a day, so there is no excuse not to do this.

If you miss one day, it's not the end of the world. But DO NOT miss two days in a row.

Progress over perfection.

Don't overthink this.

Just do it.

Step 3: Upgrade Your Expertise

> *"I can tell the level of a leader by how insatiable they are about learning."*
>
> *-Joseph Rodriques*

Leaders are readers.

Leaders are learners.

Spend 15 minutes a day on upgrading your expertise.

These can be leadership books, parenting books, personal development books, etc.

Ways to do this:

Books.

Audiobooks.

Podcasts.

Articles.

Documentaries.

Time with a mentor or coach.

Studying and modeling those who have achieved the success you desire.

> *"Knowledge is the ultimate weapon."*
> *-Jocko Willink, ret. Navy SEAL commander*

In summary, figure out the best way for you to consume information and do that.

15 minutes a day.

Don't miss two days in a row.

Don't overthink this.

Just do it.

> *"Imagine what is possible if you read a biography every day for 20 minutes of all the greatest people in history, learning from the masters, and what your life would look like in a year. Versus mindlessly scrolling through videos online."*
>
> *-Jim Kwik*

Summary

> *"The most important aspect of any organization is how it treats its people."*
>
> *-Bill Walsh*

The Three Steps to Win the Day as a leader:

1. ENERGIZE and prioritize your #1 Performance Enhancer.

2. Have ONE Three-Minute Magic Conversation.

3. Upgrade Your Expertise for 15 minutes.

One Three-Minute Magic Conversation and "Upgrading Your Expertise" for 15 minutes are "minimum effective dosages". You WILL get positive results with little time invested. You can also increase your impact by having Magic Conversations with more than one person a day, or having a longer conversation with one individual. You can read and listen to educational materials for 60 minutes a day. The more time you spend per day on Magic Conversations and Upgrading Your Expertise, the better leader you will be. Period.

Accountability Questions you can ask yourself at the end of each day:

Did I Prioritize My Number One Energy Performance Enhancer Today?

Who Did I Serve Today Through a Sincere Conversation?

What Did I Do to Upgrade My Expertise Today?

If you commit to doing these THREE things every workday for 90 days (if you miss one day, that's okay...just don't miss two days in a row), you will be amazed by the dramatic improvement in the happiness and success of:

Yourself.

Your family.

Your team members.

Your organization.

Keep it simple. Three things.

Don't overthink this.

Just do it.

"Be patient. As long as you are studying, reflecting and trying, you are making progress. Someone walking forward in the middle of the night may not be able to see how far they've gone, but they are still making progress."

-Vernon Howard

3. The Seven Challenges That Break (Or Make) Leaders

> *"Life is 10% what happens to you and 90% how you react to it."*
>
> -Charles R. Swindoll

After 20 years of studying, practicing, and coaching leadership, the following "Seven Challenges" are the most common ones that I see leaders face:

1. "Mindless Negativity" in the organization.

2. Low-performing team members.

3. Attracting, hiring, and keeping high-performing team members.

4. Not hitting organizational and/or personal goals.

5. Not enough time in the day.

6. High levels of stress.

7. Creating more leaders.

Key Solutions Toolbox

We'll now go from the "Seven Challenges" to our 17 "Key Solutions" toolbox.

After we cover each Key Solution, we'll plug select ones into each of the Seven Challenges.

On to the key solutions:

1. Lead by Example

> *"Who you are speaks so loudly*
> *I can't hear what you say."*
>
> *-Nick Saban*

People don't do what you say, they do what they see. If you want people to treat people well, you treat people well. If you want people to be focused and disciplined, you be focused and disciplined.

Don't overthink this.

It's not that complicated.

2. Best People Setup

> *"I want to share an idea with you that can completely shift the future of your company, an idea so important that without it, there is virtually no way to build a great organization. Unbelievably, far too few businesses understand the importance of this very simple fact: the future of your company is directly tied to the quality of talent you can attract and keep."*
>
> *-John Spence*

Success is in the setup.

Who you are is who you attract.

If you want to attract focused, positive, and energized people into your organization, you, your leaders, and your culture must be focused, positive, and energized by the work you do.

Your culture must be made up of and driven by:

1. A Big Energizing Mission (energizes and pulls the organization towards it)

2. High Standards (how people perform on a daily basis)

3. High Warmth (how people treat each other)

Your leaders must have:

1. Energy. They must be energized by the work and the Big Vision of the organization. They must have the ability to energize others.

> "Motivation and energy levels have three times as much weight as physical resources."

> -Napoleon Bonaparte

2. High Standards. They must have high personal standards and have the ability to uphold high standards in others.

> "Two words: everything matters."

> -Eugene Remm

3. High Warmth. They must "Know, Care, and Believe in" their people.

> "The magic formula that successful businesses
> have discovered is to treat customers like guests
> and employees like people."

> -Tom Peters

You must look for these "Three Non-Negotiable Traits" in the people you look to hire:

1. Energized. Energized by the work and vision of your organization, and the ability to energize others.

> "You can measure attitude. Be an energy-giver,
> don't be an energy-taker."

> -Urban Meyer

2. High Personal Standards. They believe in doing what they say they're going to do, plus a little extra.

> "Be so good they can't ignore you."

> -Steve Martin

3. High Warmth. They treat others with respect and dignity, and do not communicate with "Mindless Negativity".

"One of the most important factors of success is that you perceive yourself as a helper. See yourself as a helper. Your job is to help this person improve the quality of their life for work."

-Brian Tracy

If you want to attract the best people in your field, you must have the best culture in your field. To have the best culture in your field, you must have the best leaders in your field.

3. Three-Minute Magic Conversation

> *"A coach is someone who helps you help yourself."*
> *-James Wedmore*

The following is what I call a "Three-Minute Magic Conversation" because it can be done in as little as three minutes, and when repeated daily, magic happens in as little as 30 days within any organization.

There are three steps:

1. Catch

2. Challenge

3. Cross-Examine

Catch people doing things right. Praise and compliment.

Ask your team member what the number one *challenge* they are facing is, and offer help if necessary. Or *challenge* them to do something better in a way that doesn't de-motivate them.

Cross-examine (ask questions). Learn what makes them happy, unhappy, where they've been, or where they want to go. Ask this very important question:

"What do you think?"

This could be about something in the organization or something going on in their life or the world.

Have this simple, three-step conversation with ONE team member every day. If you miss one day, just don't miss two days in a row. In as little as 30 days, a leader can completely change the morale and energy of the organization for the better.

4. 5% Method to Law of Three

> "The 80/20 Principle says that most of what we do is a complete waste of time. There a few things that are incredibly important. Most results come from very few causes."
>
> -Richard Koch

Continuously look for the 5% that can be improved in your organization. The 95% that is already going right...is already going right. It does not need your immediate attention.

The 5% that needs to be improved could be some function of the business such as customer service, marketing, hiring, etc. It can also be the 5% of team members who are underperforming (or have poor attitudes) that are affecting others. As a leader, we must continuously look for the 5% that can be improved, always and forever.

The Law of Three by Brian Tracy states that there are three inputs or individuals that are causing 90% or more of the success (or 90% of the stress) in any organization. One of those inputs or individuals is causing 50%.

When you do your 5% Method analysis with the goal of looking for aspects of the organization that are problematic, figure out your top three inputs or individuals, then narrow it down to the ONE that is causing 50% of problems or stress. Address that first, then address the other two in order of importance.

5. Don't De-motivate

> "The challenge of leadership is not how to motivate the wrong people into the right people; it's how to get the right people, and then not to do all the stupid management things that tend to de-motivate the already motivated people."
>
> *-Jim Collins*

My entire management philosophy in seven words:

Hire motivated people and don't de-motivate them.

One of the biggest secrets of leadership and management is that if you simply just *don't* de-motivate your people, the vast majority will do great work.

Motivation is overrated for leaders. Hire motivated people, and for the most part, stay out of their way.

When you do everything you can to eliminate the de-motivators in your organization, you can level up to inspiring as a leader.

Inspire. Don't try to motivate. Motivation is for kids, and even kids respond better to inspiration. Motivation is talking. Inspiring is leading by example. Inspiration comes from action.

Over the last 20 years, I have identified the following de-motivators and divided them into four categories ranked in order of negative impact:

1. Demotivating Leadership

2. Demotivating Teammates

3. Demotivating Personal Work Experiences

4. Demotivating Organizations

Leadership de-motivators have by far the most negative impact on an organization, followed by demotivating teammates.

Fortunately, you are reading a book on leadership, so hopefully, you are interested in being the "least demotivating" leader you can be.

> *"How do you hire extraordinary people? The answer is, they already work for you. You just haven't given them a pathway."*
>
> *-Daniel Burrus*

Specific De-motivators

1. Demotivating Leadership

Leadership displaying low integrity, poor morals, or poor ethics

No confidence in leadership (incompetent leadership performance)

Selfishness (only looking out for themselves)

Indecisiveness (too many decisions drag out endlessly)

Under-Communication: Leadership not explaining company actions and/or sharing company data that is useful and relevant

Energy vampire leadership (negative attitude, poor mood, unhappy, tense, stressed, and/or don't want to be there)

Lack of recourse from leadership for poor performance and/or poor attitude by team members

Leadership only trying to please everyone/be everyone's friend (instead of leading)

Out of touch (out of touch with team members, customers, organizational culture, the market, business trends, the competition, and/or the organization as a whole)

Unnecessary micro-management (after clear competence is shown by the team member)

Job insecurity (fear of losing the job for something unrelated to job performance such as the organization closing, company politics, emotional instability by leadership, etc.)

Poor daily/weekly communication efforts

Unrealistic workloads created by leadership

Unclear expectations from leadership

Ruling by fear

Not recognizing good work often enough (lack of praise, lack of catching people doing things right)

Ignoring problems, neglecting to deal with problems

Public criticism from leadership (removing a team member's dignity)

Unachievable goals or deadlines given to team members (unreasonable demands)

Implied threats from leadership

Not honoring and acknowledging creative thinking and problem-solving from team members

Favoritism (playing favorites not based on merit)

Excessive fault-finding in team members (only "catching people doing things wrong" without balancing it out with sincere praise)

Leaving out important details of a team member assignment or task that needs to be completed

2. Demotivating Teammates

Unpleasant teammates (poor attitude, gossiping, blaming, complaining, condemning others)

Conflict among team members that is not productive (organizational politics, gossip, bullying, etc.)

Lazy teammates

Unskilled teammates who are not "coached up" or held to higher standards by leadership

3. Demotivating Personal Work Experiences

Boredom (no personal progress, not enough work to do, etc.)

Feeling undervalued by leadership

No personal development opportunities to grow and learn new skills

No opportunity for advancement "up the ladder" of the organization

No new responsibilities (stagnation)

4. Demotivating Organizations

No organizational progress (lack of progress and growth of the organization as a whole)

Constantly moving goalposts (therefore, no goals are taken seriously)

No clear mission, vision, and/or goals in the organization

No clear core values that guide performance and decisions in the organization

No clear performance, communication, and/or attitude standards in the organization

Standards and core values exist, but team members are not held accountable by leadership

Standards and core values exist, but are not lived up to and exemplified by leadership

Shiny object syndrome, "flavor of the week" strategy (constantly changing organizational strategy and/or vision, leading to team member confusion, unnecessary stress, and no confidence in leadership)

> *"To win in the marketplace,*
> *you must first win in the workplace."*
> *-Doug Conant, CEO, 2001–2011,*
> *Campbell Soup Company*

In conclusion, do everything you can to identify, minimize, and eliminate team member de-motivators. Always and forever. It never stops. Accept that like you chose it.

Don't overthink this.

It's not that complicated.

6. Deep Data Diagnostics (3D)

> *"There's a great line: In God we trust,*
> *and everyone else bring data."*
> *-Joshua Kalla*

I am a firm believer that every leader and every organization on the planet should be continuously collecting anonymous data from their team members, managers, and customers.

Anonymous data collection makes it safe for people to speak freely and honestly. With one-on-one conversations, group meetings, etc., many team members will be afraid to tell you what is really going on out of fear of repercussions from their leadership (or from their teammates).

Most customers will not tell you what is truly on their minds. I saw a study many years ago that found only 1 in 26 customers will be truly honest about a negative experience with a business. The other 25 will simply do business with someone else.

How often should you distribute anonymous surveys? Anonymous customer surveys should be done 365 days a year. Anonymous team member and manager surveys can be done monthly or quarterly, but no less than bi-annually (twice per year).

A simple employee survey that you can distribute anonymously:

1. On a scale of 1-10, on average how happy are you to come to work every day?

2. What are your three biggest challenges or frustrations at work?

3. What are three ways we can improve your work experience?

4. What are three ways we can improve and grow the organization?

5. If you were the president/owner/CEO/general manager/head coach for a day, what are three most important things you would do/changes you would make to improve the organization?

What you do next with this data is crucial. Many organizations do anonymous surveys, then sit on the data for months before doing something with it, or even worse, never do anything at all.

I cannot overstate how demotivating it is to the team members who filled out the surveys, only to have nothing improved in the organization.

The leadership would have been better off not even doing the surveys at all, instead of pretending that they actually cared about what their people thought and felt. Our actions (or inactions) speak far louder than our words.

Once you get the anonymous data back, the best thing you can do is to take action on at least ONE suggestion within 72 hours. It could be removing a de-motivator. Or adding something new to improve the team member work experience. You will find that many of the same suggestions come up repeatedly, so choosing one of those will have a bigger positive impact.

One of my favorite data collection tools is the Net Promoter Score. The Net Promoter Score is an employee and customer "word of mouth" metric developed by and trademarked by Fred Reichheld, Bain & Company, and Satmetrix. It lets you know if your customer or employee will promote your business to others.

If you are not currently collecting anonymous data from your team members and customers and taking action based on what you learn, it's time to start today.

Don't wait.

Do it now.

It is one of the best things you can ever do for your team members and customers.

7. No More Mindless Negativity

> *"Georgetown professor Christine Porath found that negativity is four to seven times more powerful than positivity. And when we say things out loud, they are almost ten times more powerful than we think them. If you just took these statistics at some level...what we say out loud might be 40 to 70 times more powerful if it's negative. What if I just don't say, "I don't like working here"? I'm not saying the alternative, if just not externalizing negative things."*
>
> *-Trevor Moawad*

Mindless Negativity is one of the fastest killers of a great culture and organization.

It holds many individuals and organizations back from becoming truly great.

My definition of Mindless Negativity:

Gossiping

Complaining

Condemning

Blaming

Venting

What is the opposite of mindless negativity?

1. Relentless solution focus

2. Continuous improvement mindset

According to psychologist Dr. Richard Wiseman:

"When you gossip about another person, listeners unconsciously associate you with the characteristics you are describing, ultimately leading to those characteristics being 'transferred' to you."

Executive coach Dr. Nadine Greiner, Ph.D. on venting:

"Venting feels great in the moment, but it can actually make you feel worse in the long run. This is because venting can increase your stress and anger rather than reduce them. At the same time, venting doesn't resolve the underlying causes of your stress."

Most individuals who participate in "Mindless Negativity":

1. Have no idea how much they actually do it

2. Have no idea how destructive it is to the organization

3. Have no idea how destructive it is to their peers

4. Have no idea how destructive it is to themselves

5. Have no idea that even the people who listen to them gossip, vent, blame, condemn, or complain secretly don't want to hear it, even if they agree with what you are saying

In summary: people who communicate with Mindless Negativity have no idea how destructive it is to themselves and everyone around them.

As a leader, the first step to putting a stop to Mindless Negativity is to not participate in it YOURSELF. Lead by example.

The second step is to listen to your people to understand what their biggest challenges and frustrations are. You can do this through one-on-one conversations, group discussions, and anonymous surveys. After listening, take action on helping to remedy the biggest challenges and frustrations your people are facing. And never stop listening and taking action.

The third step is to over-communicate that "Mindless Negativity" is not an appropriate way to communicate in your organization. Statistics and quotes are persuasive. You can cite the statistics and quotes I've presented in this section on why this negative form of communication is not healthy for us as individuals. You can find your own statistics and quotes to reinforce your message. Most importantly, you must communicate over and over again that we do not communicate this way as an organization, and swiftly address those individuals who are the worst offenders.

I have found that the majority of people, when addressed individually, have no idea how much they communicate with Mindless Negativity, and how detrimental it is to their relationships and how others perceive them. Learning to communicate in a more positive way will not only improve their work experience, but it can also:

1. Reduce their stress and improve their health

2. Improve their relationships with family and friends

3. Increase their overall happiness

Have the courage to address any Mindless Negativity, starting with yourself.

8. Positive Persuasion

> *"Simplicity is the ultimate sophistication."*
>
> *-Leonardo da Vinci*

In order to persuade your team members to move in a positive direction individually and collectively, your message must be carefully crafted using a very specific three-step framework I call "Positive Persuasion".

1. Simplicity. Short and to the point. Brief and bright. Quick and positive. It should be one sentence or less (five words or less is ideal). An example: "No more mindless negativity." Short and simple sticks. Long and complex doesn't.

2. Repetition. You must over-communicate it. Your people must see it and hear it at least 17 times before it starts to sink in. When you get sick of saying it (and they get sick of hearing it), that's when it BEGINS to sink in. We all have so much "noise" in our lives, the leader has to cut through it with simplicity and repetition. Team members also have to know that you are serious, and this is not just the "flavor of the week" message.

3. Conviction. You must fully believe in the message and say it with certainty. If you are "wishy-washy" and uncertain in the message yourself, your people will hear it in your voice and see it in your eyes. They will believe in the message when YOU do.

Simplicity. Repetition. Conviction.

Don't overthink this.

It's not that complicated.

9. Future Positive Focus

> *"Change the way you look at things, and the things you look at change."*
>
> *-Dr. Wayne Dyer*

In my experience, the most successful individuals, leaders, and organizations focus on two things:

The positive

The future

How I define a positive, future-oriented focus:

Positive = Gratitude + Relentless solution focus + Positive expectations

Future = Continuous improvement mindset

If you sit in and observe a leadership/management meeting in any organization, you can quickly see where they are going by listening to what ratio they are discussing the future versus the past, and the positive versus the negative.

9:1 Future to Past

According to business expert and bestselling author, Mike Michalowicz:

"Successful people focus on the future in a 9:1 ratio to the past over the mediocre."

Eleanor Roosevelt said it best:

"Great minds discuss ideas; average minds discuss events; small minds discuss people."

Ideas = the future

Events = the past

People = mindless negativity

If you want to talk about the past, then talk about it to learn from it, not dwell in it.

Discussing the future is keeping a "How can we make tomorrow better than today?" frame of mind.

5:1 Positive to Negative

Staying focused on gratitude, solutions, and positive expectations not only creates less stress and more happiness, but it also gives you a tremendous competitive advantage.

"The magic ratio is 5:1. In other words, as long as there are five times as many positive interactions between partners as there are negative, the relationship is likely to be stable. It is based on this ratio that Dr. John Gottman is able to predict divorce."

-Anthony Tshering

Dr. Emma Seppälä discussed the serious health effects of a negative work environment in an article in Harvard Business Review:

"Research by Sarah Pressman at the University of California, Irvine, found that the probability of dying early is 20% higher for obese people, 30% higher for excessive drinkers, 50% higher for smokers, but a whopping 70% higher for people with poor social relationships. Toxic, stress-filled workplaces affect social relationships and, consequently, life expectancy."

The Pygmalion effect is the occurrence through which others' expectations of a person affect that person's performance.

Having positive expectations and belief in your people on how they will perform in the future can have a direct effect on how they perform.

As the legendary motivational speaker, Les Brown, says:

Nobody rises to low expectations.

10. Say "NO" More Often

> *"99% of all effort is wasted."*
> *-Naval Ravikant*

My time management system in one word: No.

It is a tremendous time waster to say "yes" to things that:

1. Aren't important to you

2. Don't bring you happiness or happiness to those you care about

3. Don't lead to you achieving your most important goals, and

4. Don't bring you growth

Say "yes" to things that bring you happiness, success, or growth. Say "no" to things that don't.

Billionaire, Warren Buffett, on the power of no:

"The key to success: Saying "NO" 99 times out of 100 to solicitation of your time or attention. The difference between successful people and really successful people is that really successful people say "no" to almost everything."

Don't overthink this.

It's not that complicated.

11. One MIG (Most Important Goal), One MIT (Most Important Task)

"You must be single-minded. Drive for the one thing on which you have decided."
-General George S. Patton

The secret to world-class performance and achievement:

One MIG = Most Important Goal

One MIT = Most Important Task

The two most effective time frames for goals in my experience:

90 days and five years.

I have seen individuals and organizations achieve tremendous improvements and transformations in 90 days. 90

days is also a much more "mentally accessible" time frame than one year.

An individual (or organization) can become world-class in five years. This is achieved through big vision and 100% commitment, as well as disciplined, consistent execution of a few vital tasks and functions.

World-class achievement = Big Vision + 100% Commitment + (Disciplined Consistent Execution of One or Two Most Vital Important Tasks x 5 Years)

90-day blocks x 20 = 5 years

Think big and create your five-year Most Important Goal.

Then break it down into 90-day increments.

Once you have your 90-day goal decided, you must figure out your one Most Important Task.

It is the one task (two tasks at the most) that, if you do it daily and rarely miss a day, will lead you to achieving your 90-day goal. Examples:

If your one Most Important Goal is to lose 20 pounds, your one Most Important Task is eating appropriately.

If your one Most Important Goal is to improve your family relationship at home, your one Most Important Task is to spend one hour of 100% focused, zero distractions, uninterrupted time with them daily.

If your one Most Important Goal is to improve your business sales, your one Most Important Task is to spend half your workday on your one highest-impact sales and marketing initiative.

There are many, many things you could have done to achieve each one of those goals. The key is to identify the ONE most important task that has the highest impact and repeat that daily, rarely missing a day.

Don't overthink this.

It's not that complicated.

12. One MIS (Most Important Stop)

> *"Stop doing everything that doesn't contribute to you being number one."*
>
> *-Seth Godin*

Very often, stopping something can have as much impact, if not more, than starting something does on improving our situation.

As leaders, there is always one Most Important Stop (MIS) that is holding us back the most.

It could be a bad habit, or it could be a limiting belief.

Here are some examples of common things I've seen that, when stopped, can have a tremendously positive impact.

"To-Stop" Options Success and Happiness:

Saying "yes" too often

Spending time with negative people

Limiting beliefs (I can't, I'm not good enough, etc.)

Feeling like you "have" to do something (I choose to)

Mindless negativity (gossiping, complaining, blaming, condemning, venting)

Comparing yourself to others

Excessive worrying

Holding grudges (forgive)

Letting meaningless things bother you

Overspending

Working at a job that makes you miserable

Working for a boss who makes you miserable

Working for someone you don't respect

"To-Stop" Options Relationships:

Avoiding difficult conversations

Holding in your true feelings

Being a doormat (stand up for yourself)

Being overly selfish

Always trying to prove your worth

Trying to change people

Telling people what to do

Giving unsolicited advice

Giving tacit approval

Being late

Breaking your word

Cell phone or digital distractions

"To-Stop" Options Health:

Processed sugar

Refined carbohydrates

Processed food

Liquid carbohydrates

Eating foods you know you shouldn't

Buying foods at the grocery store that you know you shouldn't eat (not having them in your house changes the environment, and environment is stronger than willpower)

Social media scrolling

Negative news watching or listening

Negative music, TV, and/or movies

Checking text messages and emails after work

Staying up late

Consuming caffeine less than 8 hours before bedtime

Just like it is incredibly powerful to have one Most Important Task to achieve you one Most Important 90-Day Goal, it can be equally (or more powerful) to have one Most Important Stop that you are focusing on for 90 days.

13. 1-2 Vital Functions + 1-2 Passionate Strengths

> *"Almost everything is non-essential."*
> *-Greg McKeown*

One of the secrets of leadership and organizational success is to know your:

1. One or two "Vital Functions" as an organization, and

2. Your one or two "Passionate Strengths" as a leader.

When Vital Functions and Passionate Strengths are properly aligned, world-class results can ensue.

Your "Vital Functions" are the one or two Most Important Tasks that move the needle and get you and your organization closer to its Most Important Goal.

Your "Passionate Strengths" are the one or two work functions that you are:

1. Passionate about

2. Naturally talented at

The ultimate goal is to match up the Vital Functions with your Passionate Strengths. This is where the magic happens.

Many people and leaders waste a tremendous amount of time trying to "fix their weaknesses" and working in areas that are not within their Passionate Strengths.

Their time would be much better spent working in the areas of their Passionate Strengths and continuously improving their performance in that narrow area. And equally as important, surrounding themselves with people who have natural Passionate Strengths in the areas where they are weak.

If there are Vital Functions in the organization that don't match up with your Passionate Strengths, you must:

1. Find someone in the organization who has a Passionate Strength in that area

2. Partner up with someone currently outside of the organization who has a Passionate Strength in that area

3. Hire someone and bring them into the organization who has a Passionate Strength in that area

Examples of this would be:

Steve Jobs partnering up with Steve Wozniak because Wozniak was a genius programmer

Bill Gates hiring Steve Ballmer because Ballmer was an expert manager

Walt Disney partnering up with Roy Disney because Roy was an expert businessman

Michael Jordan partnering up with Phil Jackson because Jackson was an expert head coach

"The way to get self-belief is to focus on an area where you actually are ideally suited to do it."

-Richard Koch

Here are some examples of what the two Vital Functions might look like for leaders in the categories of business, sport, and the military:

CEO:

1) Attracting, leading, and keeping the best talent in the field

2) Growth initiative for the organization (sales, marketing, new products, business acquisitions, smart capital allocation, etc.)

College football head coach:

1) Attracting, leading, and keeping the best coaches and players in the country

2) Football strategy (preparation the week before the game, plus in-game strategy)

Military general

1) Troop welfare (walking the "front lines", checking on and speaking with the troops and leaders "in the trenches")

2) Having a deep understanding of the strategies and tactics of war, and using that knowledge to create victories

If you don't have a "Passionate Strength" as a leader in the most important "Vital Functions", you MUST find a business partner, vice president, assistant coach, spouse, etc. to fill this gap for you. If you don't, you will never achieve high-level success as an organization.

If you want to achieve world-class success as an organization, you as a leader must understand what the one or two Vital Functions are, and make sure you and your organization strive for deep domain expertise and disciplined execution there.

14. Minimum Effective Dosage

> *"What is the one thing I can do such that by doing it everything else will become easier or necessary?"*
>
> *-Gary Keller*

In order to get the most out of our time and get the most done, we must constantly be seeking out the "minimum effective dosage" in everything we do.

According to Wikipedia, the MED is defined as "the lowest dose level of a pharmaceutical product that provides a clinically significant response in average efficacy, which is also statistically significantly superior to the response provided by the placebo."

According to serial entrepreneur and venture capitalist, Martin Tobias:

"Minimum Effective Dose is a theory that was popularized in the bodybuilding community by fitness expert Arthur Jones and popularized by lifestyle hackers like Tim Ferriss and Dave Asprey.

MED is the principle of finding the smallest dose it takes to produce an ideal outcome. Anything less than your MED won't work and anything more is a waste of time, resources, and energy."

"Perfection is achieved, not when there is nothing more to add, but when there is nothing left to take away."

-Antoine de Saint-Exupéry

As leaders, we must maximize our time. One of the most effective ways to do this is to continuously ask "What is the minimum effective dosage?" in everything we do.

15. Upgrade Your Expertise

"Knowledge is the ultimate weapon."
-Jocko Willink, ret. Navy SEAL

Knowledge is the ultimate competitive advantage.

Everyone is different, so figure out how *you* best take in new information. Examples:

Physical books

Digital books (Kindle or Nook)

Audiobooks

Podcasts

Conversations with coaches, mentors, etc.

Observing someone else in action

There is no "right or wrong way" to take in information. For example, some people cannot listen to audiobooks because they "zone out" and stop paying attention. But they *can* listen to podcasts as they are generally more entertaining and easier to digest.

Some people cannot read digital books. They enjoy having a physical copy of the book in their hands.

There is no right or wrong way to upgrade your expertise. There is only the best way that works for you. What matters is that you are striving to upgrade your leadership knowledge daily to get 1% better than yesterday.

16. Maximize Your Energy

"There are three keys to being fully charged each day: doing work that provides meaning to your life, having positive social interactions with others, and taking care of yourself so you have the energy you need to do the first two things."

-Tom Rath

In order to energize others, you must be energized yourself.

You can prioritize your "physical energy" by:

1. Getting optimal sleep (this is number one for most people).

2. Eating for energy. For some people, this is intermittent fasting for 16 hours a day. For others, it is getting a good breakfast in. There are many ways to eat for energy. Talk to a reputable nutritionist and see what works best for you. The most important thing is finding a healthy eating style that you *enjoy and you'll stick to.*

3. Movement. 30 minutes of exercise per day is a good minimum effective dosage. The most important part is finding a type of exercise you *enjoy and you'll stick to.*

4. Hydration. Being dehydrated even a little bit can lead to brain fog and crankiness. Aim to drink at least half your body weight in ounces of water per day. A 140-pound person would drink 70 ounces per day or more.

You can prioritize your "mental and emotional energy" by:

1. Getting daily solitude. Even just 15 minutes a day can go a long way.

2. Doing work that you enjoy and are passionate about.

3. Surrounding yourself with positive and supportive people.

4. Taking regular vacations to reset, recover, and repair.

5. Spending time in nature, particularly near water. Beaches, lakes, rivers, etc.

Maximize your energy so you can energize others.

An outstanding book on maximizing your energy:

The 150 Most Effective Ways to Boost Your Energy by Dr. Jonny Bowden

17. Feelings as Facts Listening

> *"The entrepreneurs that don't listen never make it. I don't care what kind of product they have in their hand."*
>
> *-Barbara Corcoran*

As leaders, we want to remove our emotions from our decision-making equation as much as possible. We want to look at the facts, get the best possible information available to us, and make sound logical decisions that are the best for our people, our organizations, our communities, and our families.

This is how we should aim to operate. But there are situations where we must practice "Feelings as Facts" heart-centered listening.

We must not only put "Feelings Over Facts". We must take this a step further and treat "Feelings as Facts".

We must never, ever, ever dismiss how our people feel about a situation in our organization.

It doesn't matter what we *think*. It matters how they *feel*.

Their perception is reality.

Their feelings are facts.

As a leader, you must sit and listen without judgment when your people are upset.

Additionally, your people may have a different opinion than yours on how to proceed. This is good. Healthy and successful organizations have conflicting opinions on a daily basis.

Your people may have access to *better* information that you don't have. No leader is "omnipotent and all-knowing". Listen and learn.

You may have access to information that your people don't have. But you may have done a poor job of sharing this information when you made a decision, so they cannot understand why the decision was made.

You may not have consulted your people on an organizational decision that would have an effect on their day-to-day work. This can cause an emotional reaction of "Feelings as Facts". If they would have had the facts and were included in the discussion, you may have been able to avoid the bad feelings.

> *It doesn't matter what you think.*
> *It matters how they feel.*

How to listen continuously and avoid bad feelings:

1. One-on-one conversations, asking the two questions: "What is the biggest challenge or frustration you are currently facing?" and "What do you think about _____?"

2. Group conversations with team members, asking the two questions: "What is the biggest challenge or frustration you are currently facing?" and "What do you think about _____?"

3. Anonymous team member surveys, asking the two questions: "What is the biggest challenge or frustration you are currently facing?" and "What do you think about _____?"

Almost all bad feelings can be avoided if the leader takes the time to listen to their people on a regular basis.

Feelings over facts.

Listen with your heart.

> *"Learn as much as you can*
> *and help as much as you can."*
> *-Dr. Marshall Goldsmith*

The Seven Most Common Challenges and the 17 Key Solutions

Now that we know the "17 Key Solutions", we can plug them into the "Seven Most Common Challenges" to give ourselves a simple and effective system and framework to solve each challenge.

The Seven Most Common Challenges:

1. "Mindless Negativity" in the organization.

2. Low-performing team members.

3. Attracting, hiring, and keeping high-performing team members.

4. Not hitting organizational and/or personal goals.

5. Not enough time in the day.

6. High levels of stress.

7. Creating more leaders.

The 17 Key Solutions:

1. Lead by Example

2. Best People Setup

3. Three-Minute Magic Conversation

4. 5% Method to Law of Three

5. Don't De-motivate

6. Deep Data Diagnostics

7. No More Mindless Negativity

8. Positive Persuasion

9. Future Positive Focus

10. Say "NO" More Often

11. One MIG (Most Important Goal), One MIT (Most Important Task)

12. One MIS (Most Important Stop)

13. 1-2 Vital Functions + 1-2 Passionate Strengths

14. Minimum Effective Dosage

15. Upgrade Your Expertise

16. Maximize Your Energy

17. Feelings as Facts Listening

Here's how they fit together to form a "problem-solution system and framework":

1. Challenge: "Mindless Negativity" in the organization

Key Solutions:

Lead by Example

Best People Setup

Three-Minute Magic Conversation

5% Rule to Law of Three

Don't De-motivate

Deep Data Diagnostics

No More Mindless Negativity

Positive Persuasion

Future Positive Focus

Feelings as Facts Listening

2. Challenge: Low-performing team members.

Key Solutions:

Lead by Example

Best People Setup

Three-Minute Magic Conversation

5% Rule to Law of Three

Don't De-motivate

Deep Data Diagnostics

No More Mindless Negativity

Positive Persuasion

Feelings as Facts Listening

3. Attracting, hiring, and keeping high-performing team members.

Best People Setup

Don't De-motivate

4. Not hitting organizational and/or personal goals.

Say "NO" More Often

One MIG (Most Important Goal), One MIT (Most Important Task)

One MIS (Most Important Stop)

1-2 Vital Functions + 1-2 Passionate Strengths

Minimum Effective Dosage

Upgrade Your Expertise

5. Not enough time in the day.

Say "NO" More Often

One MIG (Most Important Goal), One MIT (Most Important Task)

One MIS (Most Important Stop)

1-2 Vital Functions + 1-2 Passionate Strengths

Minimum Effective Dosage

Future Positive Focus

Maximize Your Energy

6. High levels of stress.

Best People Setup

No More Mindless Negativity

Say "NO" More Often

The 5% Rule to Law of Three

Future Positive Focus

Maximize Your Energy

7. Creating more leaders.

Lead by Example

Best People Setup

Deep Data Diagnostics

One MIG (Most Important Goal), One MIT (Most Important Task)

One MIS (Most Important Stop)

Upgrade Your Expertise

Summary

You now have a set of simple, practical tools to effectively handle the Seven Most Common Challenges that leaders face.

These challenges can either break, or make, leaders.

You can use the tools suggested for each challenge, choose the one or few tools that you feel you need most, or come up with your own tools and solutions.

What's most important is that you have simple tools and strategies to solve the most common challenges that come up in your leadership.

As a leader, you won't be judged by the challenge itself. You will be judged by how you *respond* to it.

> *"The opposite of love isn't hate; it's indifference."*
> -*Steven Pressfield*

4. 21 Powerful Questions

"Thinking is nothing but the process of asking and answering questions. Asking yourself positive questions on a regular basis will help you make better decisions and improve the quality of your life."

-Tony Robbins

Out of the hundreds of powerful leadership questions I have discovered, the following 21 are ones I use most often.

They will help provide you with clarity of thought and the ability to know what the next right move is.

The solutions to all of your biggest challenges are already inside of you.

The 21 Powerful Questions are divided into five important categories:

State of Mind

Clarity of Focus

Straight Line Action

Best Leadership

Clear and Simple Strategy

State of Mind Questions

1. Am I having fun?

If you are not having fun the majority of the time as a leader, you will not have the energy and clarity of mind to be effective. Energy and clarity of mind are crucial for a leader to be able to compete in the business world, ball field, or battlefield.

2. What am I grateful for?

"Gratitude" and "Negative Thoughts" cannot exist in the same space in your head. Gratitude has been shown to improve physical and mental health, as well as increase mental strength.

3. Is this thought helping me or hurting me?

A simple, straightforward question that allows us to begin to observe our thoughts. Once we are able to do that, we can start to throw out the ones that don't serve us, such as limiting beliefs and comparing ourselves to others.

4. What would the most confident version of myself do?

We all have a most confident version of ourselves inside. *Low self-esteem and fear* hold us back from succeeding more than anything else.

5. What would I do if I wasn't afraid?

We all have big things that we'd like to do, but we haven't done yet. The "invisible prison" of unjustified fears hold us back. That is until we open the unlocked door of our mental prison cell and step outside into our full potential.

Clarity of Focus Questions

6. What's the one thing?

There's always *one thing* that will have a far more positive impact than everything else combined. One goal. One daily action or habit. One thing to stop that is holding you back the most. One mentor. One book. One relationship. Always look to narrow it down to the one thing that will have the biggest positive impact.

7. What's the single hardest thing I can do?

The single hardest thing is always the right thing to do in any situation. The *one emotionally most difficult thing*. Going to the gym when you don't feel like it. Asking for a raise at work, or a loan to start a business. Having a difficult conversation with someone you care about. Make the hard choice every day and watch your confidence, success, and happiness grow exponentially.

8. How simple can I make this?

Simplicity leads to results. Complexity leads to confusion. Simplicity creates success. Complexity causes a lack of execution. *Always look to simplify.*

9. If I only had two hours a day to work, what would I do?

This focusing question leads to figuring out the work that has the highest impact on achieving your goal. For most people, *80% of the workday* is not moving them efficiently and effectively closer to their most important goal.

10. Is this getting me closer to my most important goal, or farther away?

Another lens to look at our activities. Many of our daily actions and habits are not getting us closer to our major goal.

11. Does this bring me happiness or growth?

This question can be applied to the work we do, the organization we're a part of, the relationships we're in, the food we eat, the exercise we do, etc. Everything. We must also ask ourselves: *"Do I bring others happiness and growth?"*

Straight Line Action Questions

12. What would the highest version of myself do?

We all have a strong compass inside of us that points to our highest actions. Take the time to *ask and listen* to your highest inner wisdom.

13. What would I do if I was the best in the world?

If you were the best leader, parent, spouse, business owner, athlete, etc. in the world, what would you do right now and today? How is it different from what you are currently doing?

Best Leadership Questions

14. What if everyone was just like me?

What if everyone in my family, on my team, in my organization, in my community, and in the world was just like me? Would the people be confident or fearful? Positive or negative? Calm or tense? Happy or sad? Optimistic or pessimistic? Problem-focused or solution-oriented? Giving or taking? Emotions and mindsets are contagious, much more so when you are in a position of leadership. You are always under the microscope. *Live and lead by example.* Be what you want to see.

15. Who can I serve?

Personal success, organizational success, leadership success, good relationships, and happiness all have one common thread that runs through them: Service.

Clear and Simple Strategy Questions

16. What am I doing differently than those around me?

What are we doing differently than our competitors and the organizations around us? Same is lame. I have a simple rule I try to live by: If you do the opposite of what the majority are doing in any given situation, market, etc., you'll have success the majority of the time.

17. What's it gonna take to be the best?

What's it gonna take to be "best-in-class"? I learned this question from Jon Spoelstra, one of the best business leaders and marketers in the country and author of "Marketing Outrageously". If you ask yourself this simple question as an individual or organization every single day, the right answers will manifest. How many organizations are asking themselves this question daily? Very, very few.

18. How can I achieve my ten-year goal in one year?

This question is based on Parkinson's Law: "Work expands to fill the time it is given." The solution: give it less time. By giving your goal dramatically less time, you will eliminate the 95% of activities that don't truly have a big positive effect, and focus on the vital few that actually do.

19. Knowing what I know now, would I do this or start this again?

This question is based on the concept of "Zero-Based Thinking" by Brian Tracy. "If I never started this in the first place, would I do it again now? Knowing what I do now, would I still make the same decision?" If the answer is no, it's time to get out as soon as possible. This is a simple and ultra-effective litmus test. You can apply this thinking to your life, your job, a habit, your career, your business, etc.

20. If the challenge I am facing was happening to someone else, what advice would I give them?

This removes all of the emotions and tunnel vision that you have because you are personally involved. It bypasses the emotion and fear, and taps into your inner wisdom.

21. What advice would I get from my 100-year-old self?

This also removes all of the emotions and tunnel vision that you may have because you are personally involved in a situation, and taps into your inner wisdom.

Summary

The 21 Powerful Questions:

1. Am I having fun?

2. What am I grateful for?

3. Is this thought helping me or hurting me?

4. What would the most confident version of myself do?

5. What would I do if I wasn't afraid?

6. What's the one thing?

7. What's the single hardest thing I can do?

8. How simple can I make this?

9. If I only had two hours a day to work, what would I do?

10. Is this getting me closer to my most important goal, or farther away?

11. Does this bring me happiness or growth?

12. What would the highest version of myself do?

13. What would I do if I was the best in the world?

14. What if everyone was just like me?

15. Who can I serve?

16. What am I doing differently than those around me?

17. What's it gonna take to be the best?

18. How can I achieve my ten-year goal in one year?

19. Knowing what I know now, would I do this or start this again?

20. If the challenge I am facing was happening to someone else, what advice would I give them?

21. What advice would I get from my 100-year-old self?

"Research shows that asking questions improves learning and performance by as much as 150 percent."

-Gary Keller

5. The Seven True Tests of a Leader

> *"The fact is, if you want to be someone, you have to start acting that way now. You don't plan for it. You act that way immediately."*
>
> *-Alan Weiss*

Over the years, I have identified seven tests that the best leaders consistently pass. "The Seven Tests of the Best". If you can pass them consistently, world-class results will inevitably follow.

If you pass, your people will be happier and more successful. What could be better than that?

The tests are so simple, you can start applying the mindsets and habits to pass them today.

Here are the straightforward "Seven Tests of the Best". I'll present them to you in the form of questions.

1. Do we win? Do I create positive change?

2. Do I energize others? Am I still a cheerleader, coach, and mentor even on the days that I don't feel up to it?

3. Do I create more leaders?

4. Do I take 100% responsibility for the organization?

5. Does my leadership attract (and keep) great people?

6. Do I stand up for my people?

7. Do I have difficult conversations on a regular basis?

Let's go into full detail.

1. Do we win? Do I create positive change?

> *"Winning isn't everything, it's the only thing."*
> *-Vince Lombardi*

Do I win? = Can I enact positive changes that allow our people and organization to achieve a quantifiable goal?

To achieve a "win" it may take a week, a month, a year, or a decade. What you're looking for is consistent positive progress toward achieving your goal. The direction you are moving in is far more important than the exact finishing point.

Your definition of the "win" is specific to your organization and your leadership.

Examples:

Become number one in your field or market

Win a "best of" award

Customer happiness metrics

Employee happiness metrics

Survive a crisis

Achieve a yearly sales goal

Acquire or start a new business

Develop ten new leaders in the next six months

Defeat a competitor

Win a competition

Win a championship

Jocko Willink, retired Navy SEAL commander, leadership consultant, and author of the bestselling book "Extreme Ownership" on success:

"The only meaningful measure for a leader is whether the team succeeds or fails. For all the definitions, descriptions, and characterizations of leaders, there are only two that matter: effective and ineffective. Effective leaders lead successful teams that accomplish their mission and win. Ineffective leaders do not."

If you can't win as a leader, *are you really a leader yet*? Passing the next six tests are exactly what will help you win.

"When you walk in the door, there's a big sign in most of the businesses I'm involved in: What gets measured gets accomplished. Without measurement,
you're just fooling yourself."

-Dan Peña

2. Do I energize others? Am I still a cheerleader, coach, and mentor even on the days that I don't feel up to it?

> *"Life is math: In every situation, your presence either adds to or subtracts from."*
>
> *-Larry Winget*

Very few leaders can truly energize on the days they don't feel like it.

Things that cause a leader "not to feel like it":

Minor illness

Poor sleep

Poor nutrition

Lack of exercise

Family or relationship problems

Money problems

General life stress

Poor time management skills

Feelings of overwhelm

Etc.

Jocelyn Kung, leadership and organizational coach for Apple, Microsoft, and other top technology companies, on being under what I call the "leadership microscope":

"As CEO, everything you say and do is observed in detail; people attach all kinds of meaning to your words and actions. With every small movement, your tail whipsaws through the organization, impacting people's attitudes.

This doesn't just apply to what you are saying or doing, it refers more importantly to how you speak or act. If you make eye contact and stride confidently, people think the company is moving with you. By contrast, looking preoccupied and failing to say "hello" can create doubt.

Albert Mehrabian's study about communication might surprise you. He found that only 7% of what we communicate is in words. Tone is 38%, and up to 55% is in body language. Awareness of your personal presence, the ripple effect of your actions and attitudes and how people are reacting are critical to leadership."

Guess what?

No one cares that you're tired or have a cold, that you had an argument with your significant other, that you had to work extra hours this weekend, or that you got a $600 bill from your auto mechanic. They have their own problems. Everyone has problems. Your team members don't want to hear about yours. They just want you to *lead*.

Leadership is part theatre. Act like you're energized and healthy when you're around your people, no matter how you might feel inside.

That's what separates the professional leader from the amateur. The professional can energize on the days they don't feel like it.

"There is nothing more magnetic in any business field than enthusiasm and confidence."

-Barbara Corcoran

3. Do I create more leaders?

> *"You are either a multiplier*
> *or diminisher to the people in your life."*
> *-Jay Abraham*

This is easily one of the ultimate tests of a leader. If you can create more leaders, you are absolutely in the top 1% of leaders on the planet.

Four Steps to Create More Leaders

1. *Live by example* and push *yourself* to be a better leader every day. Inspire greatness in others through your own leadership mindsets and behaviors. This is most important.

2. Success is *95% in the setup*. Know what someone who has great leadership potential looks like. Example traits of high potential leaders:

Coachable. No further explanation needed.

Understand the power of commitment. They are fully committed to becoming a better leader, and also fully committed to achieving their personal goals and the goals set by the organization.

Respected. People already respect them, look up to them, and admire them, even if they don't have a leadership title yet. This is absolutely crucial.

The confidence to be respectfully honest with everyone around them, including their superiors.

Narrow focus. This is the ability to consistently focus on the one or two most important things in any given situation.

A relentless solution focus and continuous improvement mindset.

Expert listener.

Clear integrity. They do things legally, morally, and ethically. They keep their word. They don't "kick down" at others.

Energized by the work of the organization, and they have the ability to energize others.

3. *Learn how to be a great coach*. Study great coaches and people developers in multiple areas. From sports to business, to the military. Be a "Straight Shooter" in areas the leader you are coaching needs to improve on, and be a "True Believer" in their capacity for greatness. Great coaches are great listeners. Ask people what their number-one leadership challenge is, and help them work through it.

4. Schedule regular, one-on-one conversations with the leaders you are helping to develop. Be on time for these sessions, do not cancel them unless it is an emergency, and be completely focused during the session (no interruptions or digital or people distractions). This lets the person know that they (and their leadership development process) are very important to you.

Summary of the Four Steps to Create More Leaders:

1. Live by example and push yourself to be a better leader every day.

2. Success is 95% in the setup. Know what someone who has great leadership potential looks like.

3. Learn how to be a great coach.

4. Schedule regular, one-on-one conversations with the leaders you want to develop.

> "I am a huge advocate of always leaving people with better energy and feeling better than they had before."
>
> -Baron Cruz

4. Do I take 100% responsibility for the organization?

> "Yesterday I was a fool and I tried to change the world. Today I was wise so I changed myself."
>
> -Jason Demakis

We can either look at the world through a mirror or a window.

If we look at it through a window, we blame all our problems and challenges on the world.

If we look at it through a mirror, we take responsibility for our problems and challenges, and therefore, have an opportunity to solve them.

Amateur leaders blame others for their problems, challenges, and failures. They blame:

Their employees

Their players

Their managers

Their assistant coaches

Their bosses

The competition

The economy

The politicians

The weather

Their family members

Etc.

It is completely useless as a leader to blame your employees, players, managers, or assistant coaches for organizational failures.

Who hired them? You did. Who trained them? You did. Who coached them? You did.

If you are blaming any of these people for your failures, I have four words for you:

Look in the mirror.

Scott Adams, bestselling author of "How to Fail at Almost Everything and Still Win" on blaming:

"One of the key differences between successful and unsuccessful people is who do they blame. Successful people blame themselves, period. People who feel like they have control over their life and their environment will act that way, and that's a really predictable variable for success."

The professional takes 100% responsibility for everything that goes wrong because they know it is the most empowering and useful mindset they can have to solve problems and achieve success.

The professional also gives all the credit to others when things go right.

Take responsibility when things go wrong.

Give credit when they go right.

No further explanation needed.

"We're so anxious to change everything around us. Our car, our house, our neighborhood, our politicians, our iPhone, our spouse, our TV channels, our appliances. Leo Tolstoy said, "Everyone thinks of changing the world, but no one thinks of changing themselves." To take it to another level: personal change, on a scalable basis, is the real building block of lasting social change."

-Nick Seaver

5. Does my leadership attract (and keep) great people?

"Show that you are competent. Your players and staff must have the repeated experience of seeing you do your job well. They must see you prepared for your meetings with them, and see you do your own job with the highest effort and dedication."

-Urban Meyer

If I never met a leader, I could tell almost everything I'd need to know about them by the five to ten people they surround themselves with most.

If it was a company president, his or her vice presidents. If it were a head coach of a team, his or her assistant coaches.

Are those vice presidents or assistant coaches positive...or mindlessly negative?

Are they givers or takers?

Are they focused or scattered?

Are they results-driven or not?

Are the right performance metrics important to them or not?

Are they moral and ethical, or do they dismiss those concepts?

Do they have a sense of urgency, or is there no rush?

These criteria will apply all the way down to the newest employee or team member.

As a leader, we attract who we are. Period.

A-players don't want to work for B-players. People who are committed to doing great work and treating others well will not stay in an organization where the leader is not fully committed to the same.

A true sign of poor leadership is when great people are leaving an organization for the same level (or a lower) of opportunity and pay in another organization.

If you want to succeed and win as a leader, you must be the type of person that attracts and keeps great people in your organization.

"People tend to gravitate towards higher energy. They gravitate towards energy and positivity."

-Owen Cook

6. Do I stand up for my people?

> *"What you are speaks so loudly*
> *I can't hear a word you are saying."*
>
> *-Ralph Waldo Emerson*

You can tell your people that you "have their back" all day long.

Save your breath.

The only thing that they care about is if you actually have their back when it matters. This means having their back when they are attacked or mistreated by someone outside (or inside) the organization.

This could come in the form of you standing up to a rude customer who is verbally abusing your team member for no reason, when your team member was in the right. No, the customer is not always right. And yes, it is okay to fire customers sometimes.

This could be you pushing back on the media for unfairly attacking a player on your sports team. This could be you removing a talented vice president in your company because they publicly chastise, step on, and de-motivate their team members.

This could be, at the risk of you being fired, standing up for your team members to YOUR boss because your superior has created a useless new policy that serves no positive purpose other than to severely de-motivate your whole team.

Do you stand up for your people when they are mistreated? Don't tell your people you have their back. Save the "virtue signaling".

Don't say it. Be it. As long as they are doing the right thing, have your people's back when it counts.

"People do not experience your intentions;
they experience your behavior."

-Urban Meyer

7. Do I have difficult conversations on a regular basis?

> *"Caring is about valuing the person. Candor is about valuing the person's potential."*
>
> *-Mark Cole*

Do you have the ability to challenge your people to be better on a regular basis, without demotivating them or robbing them of their dignity?

Do you have the ability to:

Have *performance improvement conversations* that aren't *confrontations*?

Have *discourse* without being *disrespectful*?

Create "*emotional discomfort*" for the purpose of helping someone *grow* as a person?

I have found that if a leader truly cares about the success and happiness of someone, that person will give their leader "permission" to challenge them about attitudes or performance that does not match up with their potential as a human being.

Retired U.S. Marine general and former Secretary of State, James Mattis, on caring and criticism:

"To quote Teddy Roosevelt, "Nobody cares how much you know, until they know how much you care."

When your Marines know you care about them, then you can speak bluntly when they disappoint you.

Be honest in your criticism, but blow away the bad behavior while leaving their manhood intact."

Sometimes tough love is the best love. Developing a combination of deep care, *plus* the ability to consistently challenge your people to be their best, is one of the truest tests of a great leader.

"Total honesty at all times. It's almost always possible to be honest and positive."

-Naval Ravikant

BONUS Test

8. How much unpaid work are you willing to do to become very successful?

"Here's to those unknown and thankless hours, days, months and years of lonely hardship. What you do onstage belongs to the world; but those countless hours of unwitnessed and unappreciated preparation are yours and yours alone. They, not the stage, represent your true character."

-John Danaher, Brazilian Jiu-Jitsu Black Belt

How much work that is not directly attached to a paycheck are you willing to put in to achieve the goal of becoming one of the best at what you do?

Much of this unpaid work falls under the categories of 1) Self-education and 2) Daily practice.

John Spence, one of the top business leadership experts in the world, on the "7x1x7 Rule":

"Reading seven days per week for one hour per day in your chosen field will make you an international expert in seven years."

Brian Johnson, peak performance expert and creator of the brilliant "Optimize" YouTube channel, tells a story about the late Kobe Bryant:

"Elite performers know that they can have pretty much whatever they want if they are willing to pay the price.

"When Kobe Bryant wanted to be the best three-point shooter he could be, he made 1300 three pointers every day during the off-season.

What do you want in your life, do you believe you can have it if you pay the price, and what is the price you are willing to pay?"

Kobe Bryant described what he called his "Mamba Mentality":

"Wake up every morning trying to be better today than you were yesterday."

That is a 1% Warrior. One percent better than yesterday.

How many unpaid hours of study and practice are you willing to put in to get 1% better than yesterday?

Over and over and over again, I have seen those who are willing to:

1. Put in the most unpaid hours learning and practicing with no clear and direct payoff, and

2. Wake up every morning trying to be a little better than they were yesterday

Eventually achieve elite-level success.

Unpaid study and practice plus a continuous improvement mindset are two true hallmarks of greatness.

"Treat the first three years in any business like grad school. Be prepared to just get by and not make money. Soak up as much information you can, really learn, and do all the grunt work. Three years and one day, you'll be so far ahead of everybody else who just did it for the money, and you'll be that much more successful."

-Ryan Serhant

Chapter Summary

Here are the straightforward "Seven Tests of the Best".

1. Do we win? Do I create positive change?

Do I win? = Can I enact positive changes that allow our people and organization to achieve a quantifiable goal?

To achieve a "win", it may take a week, a month, a year, or a decade. What you're looking for is consistent positive progress toward achieving your goal. The direction you are moving in is far more important than the exact finishing point.

2. Do I energize others? Am I still a cheerleader, coach, and mentor even on the days that I don't feel up to it?

Very few leaders can truly energize on the days they don't feel like it.

No one cares that you're tired or have a cold, that you had an argument with your significant other, that you had to work extra hours this weekend, or that you got a $600 bill from your auto mechanic. They have their own problems. Everyone has problems. Your team members don't want to hear about yours. They just want you to *lead*.

3. Do I create more leaders?

This is easily one of the ultimate tests of a leader. If you can create more leaders, you are absolutely in the top 1% of leaders on the planet.

Four Steps to Create More Leaders:

1. Live by example and push yourself to be a better leader every day. Inspire greatness in others through your own leadership mindsets and behaviors. This is most important.

2. Success is 95% in the setup. Know what someone who has great leadership potential looks like.

3. Learn how to be a great coach. Study great coaches and people developers in multiple areas. From sports to business, to the military. Be a "Straight Shooter" in areas the leader you are coaching needs to improve on, and be a "True Believer" in their capacity for greatness. Great coaches are great listeners. Ask people what their number-one leadership challenge is, and help them work through it.

4. Schedule regular, one-on-one conversations with the leaders you are helping to develop. Be on time for these sessions, do not cancel them unless it is an emergency, and be completely focused during the session (no interruptions or digital or people distractions). This lets the person know that they (and their leadership development process) are very important to you.

4. Do I take 100% responsibility for the organization?

We can either look at the world through a mirror or a window. If we look at it through a window, we blame all our problems and challenges on the world. If we look at it through a mirror, we take responsibility for our problems and challenges, and therefore, have an opportunity to solve them.

5. Does my leadership attract (and keep) great people?

If I never met a leader, I could tell almost everything I'd need to know about them by the five to ten people they surround themselves with most. If it was a company president, his or her vice presidents. If it were a head coach of a team, his or her assistant coaches.

6. Do I stand up for my people?

You can tell your people that you "have their back" all day long. Save your breath. The only thing that they care about is if you actually have their back when it matters. This means having their back when they are attacked or mistreated by someone outside (or inside) the organization.

7. Do I have difficult conversations on a regular basis?

Do you have the ability to challenge your people to be better on a regular basis, without demotivating them or robbing them of their dignity?

BONUS Test

8. How much unpaid work are you willing to do to become very successful?

How much work that is not directly attached to a paycheck are you willing to put in to achieve the goal of becoming one of the best at what you do? Much of this unpaid work falls under the categories of 1) Self-education and 2) Daily practice.

6. Goal Mastery

In my previous book, "1% Warrior: The Code of Success", we covered what I have found to be the simplest and most effective goal achievement system in existence.

I call it "The Goal System That Never Fails".

It is a four-step process to achieve any SMART goal you can imagine.

SMART goals:

Specific

Measurable

Attainable

Relevant

Time Sensitive

Specific = Clearly identified

Measurable = Quantifiable and trackable

Attainable = Realistic with the tools and resources you have

Relevant = Aligns with what is really important to you

Time Sensitive = A specific timeframe and deadline

Your most important goals as a leader can be personal, professional, and preferably...both. Our personal and professional lives are connected. They do not exist separately and individually in a vacuum.

Here's the awesomely simple and effective 1% Warrior "Goal Mastery System":

Step 1: Set ONE 90-day MIG (Most Important Goal).

Step 2: Make a list of 10 to 20 activities that you can do to achieve that goal. Narrow it down to the ONE highest-impact activity, your One MIT (Most Important Task). Do this one thing every day for 90 days. If you miss a day, it's okay. Just don't miss two days in a row.

Step 3: Make a list of 10 to 20 things that you are doing that are holding you back from achieving your goal. It could be a habit or a limiting belief. Narrow it down to the ONE highest-impact thing to stop that is holding you back the most, your One MIS (Most Important Stop). Focus on that for the next 90 days.

Step 4: Find your MIP (Most Important Person) to help you achieve your goal. It could be a coach, mentor, model, friend, family member, trainer, therapist, etc. It could be an accountability partner who you will check in with and report to that you are sticking to your One MIT. This could be a friend, family member, co-worker, coach, mentor, therapist, etc.

That's all.

It works.

One goal.

One highest-impact activity to achieve that goal.

One habit to stop that is holding you back the most.

One person that can help you the most.

Don't overthink this.

It's not that complicated.

You got this.

Let's cover in more detail the four-step process of the 1% Warrior Goal Mastery System.

One Most Important Goal (MIG)

> *"Genius is obsession in one area."*
> *-Chris Eubank, Sr., former WBO middleweight and super-middleweight boxing world champion*

I love the 90-Day goal time frame.

90 days is not too long that it is overwhelming and too far into the future like a one-year goal can feel like.

90 days is not too short that it is hard to make a large improvement (although it is certainly possible to do so in 30 or 60 days, depending on the size of the goal and how committed the individual or organization is).

I have seen individuals and organizations accomplish tremendous things in 90 days, from losing a large amount of weight and dramatically improving their health to turning around a toxic workplace organizational culture.

We'll now figure out what your most important goal is for the next 90 days.

There are many ways to figure out what your one Most Important Goal is. This is one I have found useful.

Step One: Rate yourself on a scale of 1 to 10 in the following three areas, with 10 being best. This rating is your overall life satisfaction in that area:

Health (Fitness, Pain or Discomfort, Mental and Physical Health, etc.)

Wealth (Career and Personal Finances)

Relationships (Friends, Family, Co-Workers)

Now that you have given yourself a score for each one, take the area that has the lowest score and prioritize that for our 90-day Most Important Goal category.

For example, if your scores look like this:

Health score: 5 out of 10

Wealth score: 7 out of 10

Relationships score: 8 out of 10

You might pick "Health" as your area of focus.

Step 2: Put two minutes on a timer and write down as many 90-day goals as possible in the area of health that could raise your rating score on a 1 to 10 scale after 90 days.

Examples:

Lose ten pounds

Get eight hours of quality sleep per night

Fit into the pants size you wore your senior year in high school

Put on five pounds of muscle

Complete a 5k race

Get a Pink Belt in Gracie Jiu-Jitsu Women's Empowerment self-defense training

A secret: If you gave yourself two minutes or two hours to come up with these goals, you would essentially come up with the same list. You already know where you're lacking and what you have to do about it because you've most likely thought about this for a while.

Step 3: Ask yourself: if I could only achieve one goal on this list in 90 days, which one would have the biggest overall positive impact on my life?

Choose that ONE Most Important Goal and throw all the rest away.

Don't overthink this.

Just do it.

In the next section, we'll figure out the exact ONE Most Important Task you need to do to achieve your new ONE Most Important Goal.

"You should always be suspicious of complicated things. You should be even more suspicious of people who make simple things complicated."

-Perry Marshall

Here are some examples of getting crystal clear on their ONE Most Important Goal (MIG) from some of the highest achievers on the planet:

Bill Gates: A Computer with Microsoft Windows in Every Home

Elon Musk: Colonize Mars

Martin Luther King Jr.: End Racial Discrimination and Segregation in the United States

John F. Kennedy: Put a Man on the Moon

Barack Obama: Become U.S. President

Bruce Lee: Become the Biggest Movie Star in the World

Chris Guillebeau: Visit Every Country on Earth

Nate Damm: Walk Across America

James Lawrence: 50 Ironman Triathlons in 50 Days in 50 Different States

Conor McGregor: Become UFC Champion

Michael Jordan: Become NBA Champion

Kobe Bryant: Become the Greatest Basketball Player on the Planet

Arnold Schwarzenegger: Become Mr. Olympia

Arnold Schwarzenegger: Become the Biggest Movie Star in the World

Arnold Schwarzenegger: Become Governor of California

These major goals were all achieved by breaking things down into smaller time frames (example: 90 days), and laser focusing on the small handful of Most Important Tasks to get them there.

One Most Important Task

> "How do we learn how to do simple better?"
> -Joe Maddon, 2x MLB World Champion manager

Now that we are crystal clear on our ONE Most Important Goal for the next 90 days, we will now figure out the ONE highest-impact task that we need to do to give us the best chance of success.

Here are more examples of the "One Most Important Task" of world-class achievers across many categories:

Billionaire Warren Buffett: Six Hours of Reading Per Day

Founder of Walmart, Sam Walton: Modeling the Success of Other Retailers

Billionaire founder of Keller-Williams Real Estate, Gary Keller: Write a Book to Help Real Estate Agents Succeed

Joel Osteen, pastor of Lakewood Church, the largest congregation in America: Writing and Performing Sermons

Aaron Doughty, YouTube creator with one million subscribers: Create One YouTube Video Per Day

Georges St. Pierre, Two-Weight UFC mixed martial arts world champion: Seeking Out and Learning from The Best Coaches in the World

Michael Phelps, the most successful and most decorated Olympian of all time: Swim Six Hours a Day

Legendary college football coach, Nick Saban: Recruiting the Best Players and Coaches

Billionaire investor, Jim Simons: Hiring the Best People

Billionaire founder of Microsoft, Bill Gates: Hiring the Best People

United States Marine General and former Secretary of Defense, James Mattis: Troop Welfare

Legendary comedian, Jerry Seinfeld: Writing Jokes Every Single Day (Don't Break the Chain)

Billionaire founder of Amazon, Jeff Bezos: Customer Obsession

"Bill Gates has said that if you took the twenty smartest people out of Microsoft it would be an insignificant company, and if you ask around the company what its core competency is, they don't say anything about software. They say it's hiring."

-Geoff Colvin

One Most Important Task Exercise

We'll now figure out what your ONE Most Important Task is for the next 90 days for the ONE Most Important Goal you chose in the last exercise.

> *"What's the one thing I could do every single day, that a year from now, I would totally change my life?"*
>
> *-Aaron Doughty*

Step 1: Put two minutes on a timer and write down as many tasks as possible you could do to achieve your ONE Most Important Goal in 90 days.

Example tasks if your goal was to lose 10 pounds in 90 days:

Get eight hours of quality sleep per night

Run for three miles every day

Hire a personal trainer to create a seven-day per week exercise routine for you

Get a workout buddy to exercise with you every day

Clean up your nutrition/diet by reducing calories and/or sugars

Step 2: Ask yourself: if I could only do ONE thing on this list for 90 days, which one would have the biggest overall positive impact on me achieving my ONE Most Important Goal? Choose that ONE Most Important Task, put 90% of your focus on that for the next 90 days, and don't miss two days in a row.

> *"The 80/20 Principle says that most of what we do is a complete waste of time. There a few things that are incredibly important. Most results come from very few causes."*
>
> *-Richard Koch*

With our example tasks above for the goal of losing ten pounds, the ONE best choice would be "Clean up your nutrition/diet by reducing calories and/or sugars".

The vast majority of health and fitness experts would agree with this.

You may have heard such fitness industry sayings such as "You can't outwork a bad diet" and "Abs are made in the kitchen".

The other four tasks on the list we made above are certainly useful and can lead to overall improvement in mental and physical health.

But if we could ONLY choose one for the goal of losing ten pounds, it's the nutrition choice, hands down.

Keep it simple.

Don't overthink this.

Just do it.

> *"98% of business owners fail because they aren't able to focus for 3-5 hours a day, uninterrupted, on the one most important thing. Don't worry about a bunch of business tactics, just pick one and do it every day for a few hours. Those who are able to focus the longest and also delay gratification the longest are the most successful in life. Look at pro athletes and Steve Jobs and other billionaires. They are psychopaths with this stuff. They cut everything else out and focus."*
>
> *-Alex Becker*

Habit Mastery

Once you figure out the ONE Most Important Task you have to do every day, here are five ultra-powerful tips on how to keep your new One MIT habit going:

1. Keep focusing on your new One MIT habit for at least 66 days.

Dr. Phillippa Lally of the University College London conducted a study with her team to figure out how long it actually takes to form a habit. According to her study that was published in the European Journal of Social Psychology, it took anywhere from 18 days to 254 days for individuals to form a new habit, with the average time being 66 days.

2. Build one new habit at a time. At the VERY most, two new habits. If you feel extremely "Locked In" on your new habit after two or three weeks (around 18 days), you can add a second habit.

3. Start smaller than you think. Don't set the bar too high in the beginning. Make it as easy as possible. Instead of trying to write for three hours a day, start with just 30 minutes. Instead of trying to walk for an hour a day, start with 15 minutes.

4. Daily check-ins with an Accountability Partner can double your chances of forming and sticking to your new One MIT habit. Get yourself one.

Peak performance coach, Mandy Schumaker, summarizes a study by the American Society of Training and Development (ASTD) about the probability of completing a goal:

"You hear an idea (10%)

You consciously decide to adopt it (25%)

You decide when you will do it (40%)

You plan how you will do it (50%)

You commit to someone else you will do it (65%)

You have specific accountability appointments with the person(s) committed-95%

Accountability programs, like engaging a daily accountability partner will DOUBLE your success rate."

5. Don't miss two days in a row of your new MIT habit. We're not robots, so if we miss one day, it's not the end of the world. Progress over perfection. Just don't miss two. According to Dr. Phillippa Lally's study on habit formation, missing a single day did not reduce the chance of forming a habit.

"Never let two days in a row go by without doing something towards your goal."

-Brandon Turner

In summary:

1. Keep focusing on your new One MIT habit for at least 66 days.

2. Build one new habit at a time. At the VERY most, two new habits.

3. Start smaller than you think. Don't set the bar too high in the beginning.

4. Daily check-ins with an Accountability Partner can double your chances of forming and sticking to your new One MIT habit.

5. Don't miss two days in a row of your new MIT habit. We're not robots, so if we miss one day, it's not the end of the world.

Keep it simple.

You got this.

One Most Important Stop (MIS)

> *"Half the leaders I have met don't need to learn what to do. They need to learn what to stop. We get credit for doing something good. We rarely get credit for ceasing to do something bad. Yet they are flip sides of the same coin. Stopping some behavior gets no attention, but it can be as crucial as everything else we do combined."*
>
> *-Dr. Marshall Goldsmith*

So often, we think about progress and growth as what we need to "start" doing.

I need to start eating healthier.

I need to start exercising after work.

I need to be more positive.

I need to start saving money.

Consider another solution: doing nothing.

"Stopping" your way to success.

Instead of trying harder, consider what peak performance expert, Dr. Price Pritchett, would call "trying easier".

Start eating healthier turns into:

Stop drinking any sugary beverages like soda or fruit juice.

Start exercising after work turns into:

Stop sitting on the couch when I come home from work.

Start being more positive turns into:

Stop being mindlessly negative (gossiping, complaining, blaming, condemning, venting).

Start saving more money turns into:

Stop spending money on things I don't really need.

You get the picture now.

> *"To achieve the goal of "being nicer." All you have to do is "stop being a jerk." All you have to do is...nothing."*
> *-Dr. Marshall Goldsmith*

Peak performance expert, Brian Johnson, on the power of stopping applied to your health:

"Rule number one from Dr. Steven Gundry, author of the Plant Paradox: What you stop eating has a bigger impact on your health than what you start eating.

You can start eating a lot more broccoli or whatever you think is good for you, but if you don't stop eating that pizza, there's no amount of broccoli you're going to eat that's going to take care of all the damage you're doing from eating something that doesn't work for you."

That rule applies to everything. Peak performance expert, Dave Asprey, says: "The fastest way to boost your performance is to quit doing the things draining your energy. Whether that's your health, psychological, or relationship health and vitality. Stop doing the things that are damaging your relationships, mind, or body."

John Durant, author of the Paleo Manifesto, says: "In nature, you will never find a fountain of youth, but there are things that you can eat that will immediately kill you. Stop doing the things that are toxic if we want to optimize our well-being."

To give you some ideas on what you might want to consider stopping, here's a list I've compiled over the years from observing the "power of stopping". The "stops" are broken down for you into three categories:

1. Success and happiness

2. Relationships

3. Health

1. One Thing to Stop Success and Happiness:

Saying "yes" too often

Spending time with negative people

Limiting beliefs (I can't, I'm not good enough, etc.)

Feeling like you "have" to do something (I choose to)

Mindless negativity (gossiping, complaining, blaming, condemning, venting)

Comparing yourself to others

Excessive worrying

Holding grudges (forgive)

Letting meaningless things bother you

Overspending

Working at a job that makes you miserable

Working for a boss who makes you miserable

Working for someone you don't respect

2. One Thing to Stop Relationships:

Avoiding difficult conversations

Holding in your true feelings

Being a doormat (stand up for yourself)

Being overly selfish

Always trying to prove your worth

Trying to change people

Telling people what to do

Giving unsolicited advice

Giving tacit approval

Being late

Breaking your word

Cell phone or digital distractions

3. One Thing to Stop Health:

Processed sugar

Refined carbohydrates

Processed food

Liquid carbohydrates

Eating foods you know that you shouldn't

Buying foods at the grocery store that you know you shouldn't eat (not having them in your house changes the environment, and environment is stronger than willpower)

Social media scrolling

Negative news watching or listening

Negative music, TV, and/or movies

Checking text messages and emails after work

Staying up late

Consuming caffeine less than eight hours before bedtime

Inversion

> *"All I want to know is where I'm going to die so I don't go there."*
>
> *-Charlie Munger*

Practicing "inversion thinking" and knowing what to avoid in life is an often overlooked but incredibly powerful mental model.

Billionaire, Charlie Munger, on the success of Berkshire Hathaway:

"It's not brilliance. It's just avoiding stupidity."

According to peak performance expert, Tai Lopez, billionaire, Warren Buffet, asked the following question to an audience:

"If you could pick one person from your high school and receive 10% of their income for free for the duration of their life, who would you bet on?

You want to become the person you would bet on.

Bet against sloth and unreliability.

Bet on clarity of path and purpose at an early age and deep domain expertise."

One Most Important Stop (MIS) Exercise

> *"The real path to greatness, it turns out, requires simplicity and diligence. It requires clarity, not instant illumination. It demands each of us to focus on what is vital—and to eliminate all of the extraneous distractions."*
>
> *-Jim Collins*

We'll now figure out what your ONE Most Important Stop is for the next 90 days, that if we stopped doing that one thing, it would have a tremendously positive difference in our life and the lives of the people we care about.

Step 1: Put two minutes on a timer and write down as many things as possible that you know you need to stop doing.

Examples:

Stop mindlessly complaining

Stop drinking soda

Stop checking your cell phone after work when you want to be giving your family your full attention

Stop buying shoes and clothes that you don't really need

Step 2: Ask yourself: if I could only do ONE thing on this list for 90 days, which one would have the biggest overall positive impact on my life and the lives of the people I care about? Choose that ONE Most Important Stop, and put focus on that for the next 90 days.

Don't worry about being perfect. Progress over perfection.

Don't overthink this.

It's not that complicated.

Just do it.

> "Any time you have a big goal or ambition, ask yourself,
> "What would it look like if it were easy?".
>
> -Tim Ferriss

One Most Important Person (MIP)

> "There is a difference between interest
> and commitment. When you're interested in doing
> something, you do it only when it's convenient.
> When you're committed to something, you accept no
> excuses, only results"
>
> -Ken Blanchard

Get some help.

The last part of the formula is your One Most Important Person (MIP)

This person can be:

An accountability partner

A coach

A trainer

A mentor

Someone to model

The advice you follow from an expert's book

A physical or mental health professional

A friend or family member

> *"Always look for a teacher."*
>
> *-Ido Portal*

After more than two decades of studying the habits and mindsets of peak performance, I have discovered that there are only three shortcuts to success. They are what I call "The M3 Method:

Mentorship

Modeling

Most Impactful Books

Success leaves clues. Strive to become the ultimate "Success Detective". It is one of the best and most important things you can ever do.

The most successful people study success. Plain and simple.

As described by his biographer, Roland Lazenby, all-time NBA great and worldwide icon, Michael Jordan "asked more questions to those around him than any other player in the NBA."

Advice from peak performance and business expert, James Altucher:

"Stand next to the smartest person in the room.

Harold Ramis did it (Bill Murray).

Steve Jobs did it (Steve Wozniak).

Craig Silverstein did it (Larry Page).

Kanye West did it (Jay-Z).

I make money only when I do this."

You must do everything you can to expose yourself, study, and spend time with the kind of people you want to become. This applies to health, wealth, relationships, and happiness.

According to business expert, John Spence: "The quality of questions you ask yourself and others determines the quality of your life."

All-time great NBA champion, Kobe Bryant, in his own words:

"Basketball was the most important thing to me. Everything I saw, whether it was books I read, TV shows, or people I talked to, everything that was done was to learn to become a better basketball player. When you have that point of view, the world becomes your library to help you become better at your craft. You know what you're looking for."

Kobe's "Mamba Mentality": wake up every morning trying to be better today than you were yesterday.

Advice from retired Army Green Beret and UFC fighter, Tim Kennedy:

"If you think you're the best at what you do, you're not. Be courageous and find somebody better."

Finding a World-Class Mentor or Coach

> *"My mantra: Just do the best you can. All I can do every day is do the best I can. And learn."*
>
> *-Tom Cruise*

Here are the ten specific things I have done for the last 20 years to have access to and learn from many world-class mentors:

1. Think as big as possible and go right to the top of your field. I can promise you that almost no one is asking them. The worst thing they can say is no. But many will say yes. Be persistent.

2. If you have the means and think it is necessary, you can offer to pay for their time. Many will turn down the payment offer and mentor you for free.

3. Take action on their suggestions.

4. Start by asking for just 15 minutes of their time.

5. If they say yes, be a good and respectful student, this means: show up on time, don't cancel, and be extremely polite.

6. Have questions prepared and take notes. If you can give them the questions in advance of your conversation, even better.

7. Listen, listen, listen. Spend 99% of the conversation listening, and 1% asking questions. A huge mistake I see people make with a mentor is they talk too much or give their own opinions. That is an outstanding way to lose your mentor.

8. When finished, give a hand-written thank-you note for their time, and even a thoughtful gift down the road.

9. If you do all these things just right, many times your mentor will talk to you again. Always be respectful of their time, and don't take too much of it.

10. Another great move is to offer to volunteer your time in service to their organization in trade for their mentorship.

Peak performance expert and fitness franchise owner, Bedros Keuilian's philosophy on mentorship:

"I grow by constantly putting myself in situations with people who are better than me. I seek out people who are in better shape, making more money, or making a bigger impact in the world. I never want to be the smartest person in the room. I want to learn from people at a higher level than me so I can join them there, then repeat the whole process."

Here are ten of my favorite questions I ask a mentor or anyone I am trying to learn from:

1. What are three pieces of advice that you would give yourself when you first started out?

2. What are three big mistakes to avoid?

3. What are three pieces of life advice that you would give to your 20-year-old self?

4. What's the one most important thing you do every single day?

5. Who are your mentors?

6. What are the three best pieces of advice you've received from your mentors?

7. Who are the three individuals or organizations whom you modeled their success?

8. What are some of your favorite books or resources?

9. If you had to start from scratch and get to where you are now again as fast as possible, what are the top three most important things you would do?

10. If you could draw a simple map on a napkin to double or 10X my success, what would it look like?

There also many outstanding paid options for "mentorship" to help solve the specific challenge you might be facing:

An industry-specific business coach to help you increase profits

A life coach to help you reach a goal

A mental health professional if you are feeling depressed

A doctor to help you figure out why you are continuously tired

A personal trainer to help you get in better physical shape

A nutritionist to help you improve your health

A certified professional counselor to help you improve a relationship

Coaching and counseling is another secret weapon of the happiest and most successful people.

It is one of the best investments you can ever make.

Find a reputable one who has outstanding reviews or someone who has been referred to you by someone that you trust. This is very important.

In summary, have the courage to go out and seek the best mentor, coach, or professional counselor you can find. You can cut five to 50 years off of your learning, growing, or health curve. This is invaluable and beyond priceless.

Don't wait. Don't overthink this. Just do it.

> *"You can't be what you can't see. You must get exposed to the quality you want to have."*
>
> *-Jay Shetty*

Summary

One more time, the awesomely simple and effective 1% Warrior Goal Mastery System:

Step 1: Set ONE 90-day MIG (Most Important Goal).

Step 2: Make a list of 10 to 20 activities that you can do to achieve that goal. Narrow it down to the ONE highest-impact activity, your One MIT (Most Important Task). Do this one thing every day for 90 days. If you miss a day, it's okay. Just don't miss two days in a row.

Step 3: Make a list of 10 to 20 things that you are doing that are holding you back from achieving your goal. It could be a habit or a limiting belief. Narrow it down to the ONE highest-impact thing to stop, your One MIS (Most Important Stop). Focus on that for the next 90 days.

Step 4: Find your MIP (Most Important Person) to help you achieve your goal. It could be a coach, mentor, model, trainer, therapist, etc. It could be an accountability partner who you will check in with and report to that you are sticking to your One MIT. This could be a friend, family member, co-worker, coach, mentor, therapist, etc.

One goal.

One highest-impact activity to achieve that goal.

One habit to stop that is holding you back the most.

One person that can help you the most.

Follow these five steps to master your new "One Most Important Task" and "One Most Important Stop" habits:

1. Keep focusing on your new One MIT habit for at least 66 days.

2. Build one new habit at a time. At the VERY most, two new habits.

3. Start smaller than you think. Don't set the bar too high in the beginning.

4. Daily check-ins with an Accountability Partner can double your chances of forming and sticking to your new One MIT habit.

5. Don't miss two days in a row of your new MIT habit. We're not robots, so if we miss one day, it's not the end of the world.

That's all.

It works.

Don't overthink this.

It's not that complicated.

You got this.

1% better than yesterday.

7. Time Mastery:
The Beat the Clock System

"Until you value yourself, you won't value your time. Until you value your time, you won't do anything with it."
-M. Scott Peck

How do those with the exact same amount of time as us, 24 hours in a day, 7 days in a week, 365 days in a year, accomplish extraordinary things like becoming an Olympic athlete, graduate Valedictorian, or achieve billionaire status?

Time mastery.

It cannot be overstated how much mastering your time can have a positive effect on your health, wealth, relationships, and happiness.

The "Beat the Clock" Seven-Step Time Mastery system encompasses the mindsets and habits of the people who get the most done on the planet:

1. Maximize Your Energy

2. The Power of One (The 80/20 Principle)

3. Say "NO" to Almost Everything

4. Extreme Time-Blocking

5. Live Faster (Parkinson's Law)

6. Work in Your 1-2 Strengths (Ikigai)

7. Deep Learning (Leveraging Other People's Knowledge)

And now, the seven steps in detail.

1. Maximize Your Energy

> *"There are three keys to being fully charged each day: doing work that provides meaning to your life, having positive social interactions with others, and taking care of yourself so you have the energy you need to do the first two things."*
>
> *-Tom Rath*

In order to maximize your time, you must *maximize your energy*.

How to maximize your energy:

Eat foods that give you energy (that you also enjoy), and avoid foods that make you tired or give you "brain fog"

Get good quality sleep

Do exercise that you enjoy with people you like

Drink plenty of water

Spend time with energizing people

Eliminate (or dramatically reduce the time spent with) people who are time and energy vampires in your life

Adopt a positive morning routine/golden hour/hour of power

Focus on one thing at a time (multitasking is an energy drainer)

Do work that energizes you

Have hobbies that energize you

Do not check your cell phone for text messages or emails for the first and last hour of the day for peace of mind

Be on time (it is empowering)

Billionaires, Mark Cuban, Jeff Bezos, Jack Dorsey, and Sir Richard Branson, all prioritize their energy through exercise.

> *"The practice of being fully engaged in the thing you're doing (right now) conserves a ton of energy."*
> *-Marie Forleo*

2. The Power of One (The 80/20 Principle)

> *"Productivity can be boiled down to one word—FOCUS."*
> *-Mel Robbins*

Have ONE key, measurable, non-negotiable, high-impact goal.

Do the ONE most important, highest-impact task every day to get you closer to achieving that goal.

Spend at least half of your workday on that ONE TASK that has the biggest impact on achieving your NUMBER ONE most important goal.

Example goals:

Increasing sales by 20%

Acquiring one new breakthrough client

Reducing your work stress by 50%

Reducing your work week to four days

Identifying and developing one new leader

Figure out the ONE most important task and ALWAYS get that done. Focus like a LASER on that ONE MIT (Most Important Task), that MVP (Most Valuable Priority).

Billionaires, Elon Musk, Bill Gates, Steve Jobs, Mark Zuckerberg, Warren Buffett, Gary Keller, and Sam Walton, have all operated with "One Thing" laser-like focus in their businesses.

The 80/20 Principle, also known as the Pareto principle and "the law of the vital few", was discovered by Italian economist, Vilfredo Pareto, in 1896. "80% of outcomes (or outputs) result from 20% of all causes (or inputs) for any given event".

Quotes from thought leaders on the 80/20 Principle:

"The 80/20 Rule: 80% of the effects come from 20% of the causes. This means that if you're doing ten tasks, two are going to be vastly more important than the others."

-Brian Tracy

"20% of your activities will account for 80% of your results."

-Brian Tracy

"The 80/20 Principle, that 80% of results flow from just 20% of the causes, is one of the true principles of highly effective people." -Richard Koch, author of "The 80/20 Principle"

"20% of everything you do is responsible for 80% of your successes." -Chalene Johnson

The 80/20 Principle can be applied to anything and everything: weight loss, healthy (or unhealthy) relationships, business success, personal happiness, etc.

Having a laser-like focus on what is most important at all times is an "elusively obvious" secret of world-class achievement.

A simple, yes or no, binary question to always keep you focused on your major goal:

Is what I'm doing getting me closer to my goal, or farther away?

"Achievers always work from a clear sense of priority."

-Gary Keller

3. Say "NO" to Almost Everything

> *"If you never did 75% of what you do every day, it wouldn't matter."*
>
> *-Dan Peña*

Be incredibly lazy at the things that don't matter and incredibly disciplined at the things that do.

Practice "The Power of No". The happiest and most successful people say "NO" the most, and are continuously simplifying everything in their life and work.

"Busy" is not a "badge of honor". When someone says they are SO busy, this is what is really going on 99% of the time with that individual: "I can't consistently say "NO" to what's not important."

We don't want to be "busy". We want to be *focused and getting results*.

Say "NO" often to unnecessary or low-impact activities.

Legendary business expert, Michael Porter, puts it best: "The essence of strategy is choosing what not to do."

Once you figure out the one or two Most Important Tasks that really move the needle (that get you closer to you Most Important Goal), you need to say "NO" to almost everything else.

Peak performance expert, Tim Ferriss, author of "Tools of Titans" and "Tribe of Mentors", proposes this brilliant question:

"What if I could only subtract to solve problems? What should I put on my not-to-do list?"

Tim expands further on this concept:

"Choosing the few right things very carefully and doing them (being effective) is more important than doing a lot of things well (being efficient). Doing things well does not automatically make them important."

Make a "to stop" list of the activities that are hurting your productivity.

If it's not your one or two Most Important Tasks, do everything you can to delegate it, or don't do it at all.

Delegate anything that is not so crucially important that you do it personally to someone else who can do it *80% as good as you. In many cases, "good enough is good enough" and "done is better than perfect".*

Additionally, distractions destroy productivity. Say "NO" to and eliminate as many distractions as possible. Remove the distractions (cell phone notifications, people interruptions, etc.). Teach everyone in your life and work when and how you want to be communicated with.

Meetings

> *"A meeting is an event where minutes are taken and hours are wasted."*
> -Captain James T. Kirk

One of the most important things you can ever do is *say "no" to almost all meetings.*

Cameron Herold, author of "Meetings Suck" and the best-selling book, "Double Double: How to Double Your Revenue and Profit in Three Years or Less" and former COO of 1-800-GOT-JUNK? on meetings:

"Meetings reflect the nature of your company's culture. If you want a culture to be energetic, focused and accountable, your meetings have to embody those same characteristics. Your meetings can improve the atmosphere of the entire organization. Or they leave your company listless and without direction."

95% of meetings are a waste of time, and can easily be replaced with quick one-on-one conversations, short "huddles", brief group emails, etc.

If you are going to hold or participate in a meeting, they should be:

1. Brief. You can hold effective meetings for large organizations in as quick as 15 minutes.

2. Bright. Positive and solution-oriented. Start and end the meeting on a positive note.

3. Future-focused. Ideas and solutions. No endless "archeological digs" into the past.

4. Clear start times and end times. Start on time and end on time.

5. Clear agenda of five discussion items or less, starting the meeting with the number one most important topic of discussion.

6. The best meetings have strong "moderators" leading them, keeping everyone focused and moving.

7. Get closure on one topic before going to the next.

8. Avoid all cell phone or laptop usage unless it's absolutely to take notes or to look something up.

9. Clear action steps at the end of the meeting with specific individuals who will do the work, and also clear deadlines.

10. Figure out your best meeting cadence for your organization. For example: five-minute daily team huddles, 15-minute weekly meetings, 55-minute monthly meetings, 90-minute quarterly meetings, one-day yearly meetings.

Conclusion

> *"It is not the daily increase, but the daily decrease.*
> *Hack away at the inessentials."*
>
> *-Bruce Lee*

Parkinson's Law of Triviality: Most organizations and people will spend the most time on trivial issues and the least time on important issues.

Billionaire, Warren Buffet's key to success (in his words):

Saying "NO" 99 times out of 100 to solicitation of his time or attention.

"NO" is a complete sentence.

Saying "NO" is like exercising a muscle at the gym. The more you exercise it, the stronger it gets and the easier it is to do.

4. Extreme Time-Blocking

> *"You will need to put up barriers to protect your time so you can serve more people."*
>
> *-Russell Brunson*

Extreme time-blocking is one of the ultimate secrets of productivity.

Forget "to-do lists". They are overwhelming and stressful.

Instead, schedule all of the important things you do into your daily calendar on your phone (or a physical daily planner if you prefer). Write out your day, scheduling all activities and time-blocking everything.

We must work from a calendar, not a to-do list.

Until you get a good handle on how long your most common tasks take, add 50% to your time estimate for completing a task. If you think it will take 60 minutes, schedule 90 minutes in your calendar.

Two steps to Extreme Time-Blocking:

1. Write out your entire day in blocks of time.

2. Shorten the blocks into the smallest increments of time whenever possible and as much as possible. 30 minutes, 15 minutes, etc.

When you schedule a meeting, conversation, task, etc. in 15-minute blocks instead of one-hour blocks on your calendar, everyone involved (yourself included) will figure out how to get *right to the point* and get to the heart of the matter.

A few examples of Extreme Time-Blocking:

Warren Buffet in ten-minute increments

Bill Gates scheduled his meetings in six-minute increments.

Elon Musk schedules his day in five-minute slots

> *"A person who cannot keep appointments on time, cannot keep scheduled commitments, or cannot stick to a schedule cannot be trusted in other ways either."*
> *-Dan Kennedy*

5. Live Faster (Parkinson's Law)

> *"Success loves speed. Delay kills dreams."*
> *-Craig Ballantyne*

Having a healthy sense of urgency is one of the greatest competitive advantages in business (and life).

Focusing on being 10% more productive each day gives you over a FULL MONTH of extra productivity a year.

Parkinson's Law: "Work expands so as to fill the time available for its completion". The amount of time that one has to perform a task is the amount of time it will take to complete the task.

According to Tim Ferriss, billionaire PayPal founder, Peter Thiel, offers up a brilliant productivity question:

"If you have a ten-year plan to get somewhere, why can't you get there in six months?"

By asking this question, it forces you to *think differently*, and to eliminate any unnecessary steps in achieving your goal.

Brief and Bright

One of the most useful habits one can ever adopt to get to the top 1% of productive people is being "Brief and Bright". Be "Brief and Bright" in conversations, meetings, text messages, emails, etc. This means be *short but positive*. If I could only choose one when it comes to getting more things done, it would be "brief". If you want to also be a caring and energizing leader, you must also be "bright".

Examples of Brief and Bright used in different forms of communication:

1. Conversation: speak/make your point in under 30 seconds. Even better, in eight seconds or less (the average attention span of a human being).

2. Meetings: 15-minute weekly meetings (and only if important and necessary). Even better, daily two-minute standing huddles (everyone is standing up).

3. Text messages: no more than one sentence. Even better: three to five words.

4. Email: A few short sentences (or less). Even better, 140 characters or less.

Perfection is the Enemy of Excellence

Another ultra-useful mentality for getting to the top 1% of productive people: Done is better than perfect. Get it done. Test the results and reactions. Adjust, improve, and make corrections.

Don't let perfectionism paralyze you. Being a perfectionist can turn a project that could be completed in a week into a project still not completed in a month.

For the majority of things in life:

Good enough is good enough.

Done is better than perfect.

And progress over perfection.

> "Successful people walk 25% faster than unsuccessful people."
>
> -David Schwartz, The Magic of Thinking Big

6. Work in Your 1-2 Strengths (Ikigai)

> *"Working on your weaknesses is a huge flaw.*
> *Get great at what you're good at. We only need to be good at one or two things and we can make an impact on the world."*
> *-Dean Graziosi*

Working in the areas of your one or two biggest strengths is one of the most useful productivity tools imaginable.

You will be *happier and more successful* when you work in the areas of your natural strengths. You'll get more done in less time because you are naturally good at it. You'll get more joy out of the work you do because you are naturally inclined to it.

One of the secrets of leadership and organizational success is to know your:

1. One or two "Vital Functions" as an organization, and

2. Your one or two "Passionate Strengths" as a leader.

When Vital Functions and Passionate Strengths are properly aligned, world-class results are attainable.

Your "Vital Functions" are the one or two Most Important Tasks that move the needle and get you and your organization closer to its Most Important Goal.

Your "Passionate Strengths" are the one or two work functions that you are:

1. Passionate about

2. Naturally talented at

The ultimate goal is to match up the Vital Functions with your Passionate Strengths. This is where the magic happens.

Here are some examples from billionaires on how they work in the areas of their two biggest strengths and the two most important vital functions:

Steve Jobs = technology and sales

Mark Cuban = technology and sales

Bill Gates = technology and partnering with the best people

Warren Buffett = investing and sales

Sam Walton = studying best practices in retail and building more stores

Mark Zuckerberg = getting more users on the social media platform and partnering with the best people

Elon Musk = engineering and sales

Each had two major focuses that helped them build some of the most successful companies on the planet.

The goal of a leader is to spend at least 90% of the day on the one or two Vital Functions of the organization. The other 10% of the time can be used to address challenges that arise and new growth opportunities to investigate.

Delegation Mastery

> *"Instead of asking, "how can I do this?" ask "how can this get done?".*
>
> *-Kevin Kruse*

In order to be able to focus 90% of our day on the one or two Vital Functions of our organization that match up with our one or two Passionate Strengths, we must become "Master Delegators".

Ineffective delegation is one of the best ways I know to increase a leader's stress, and waste a ton of time on tasks that don't "move the needle" for the organization.

Seven Steps to Delegation Mastery:

1. If a team member or leader asks for the task, *give it to them.*

2. Allow people to fail safely.

3. Bring people problems, not solutions, and let them figure out their best way to solve it.

4. 10-80-10 Rule: give someone an objective/task and clearly define the process and result you are looking for (first 10%), allow them to work on the objective/task (middle 80%), then check the result and either approve or course-correct (final 10%).

5. Delegate things that people can do 80% as good as you so you can do the highest-impact work you are strongest at.

6. Delegate as much as you can that is not your expertise. Spend 90% of your time (or more) doing the highest-impact work that you are strongest at.

7. Asking for help as a leader does not make you look weak or incompetent. When done the right way, it makes you look strong and smart. Help, and ask for help, religiously.

Ikigai

Author, Anneke Kuijk, gives an outstanding description of "Ikigai", one of the most powerful concepts of success and happiness:

"'Ikigai' is a Japanese concept that, simply put, means 'your reason to get out of bed in the morning'.

"Ikigai is a combination of the words 'iki', which means life or living, and the word 'kai' (pronounced as gai), which represents value, effect, result, or usefulness.

What is 'ikigai' exactly? It is that place where your passion, mission, calling and career intersect.

This is best illustrated by the overlapping circles of a Venn diagram.

The four circles represent:

What you love

What you are good at

What the world needs

What you are/could be paid for

The place where the four circles meet, is where you find your 'ikigai'."

Summary

Figure out what your one or two Passionate Strengths are. The one or two things that come easier to you than other people, and that you love to work on and learn about.

When you are not working in the areas of your one or two Passionate Strengths, you will feel like you are meeting "resistance" and continuously "swimming upstream". When you are working in the areas of your two Passionate Strengths, you are "going with the flow" and "riding the wave".

Live in the areas of your one to two Passionate Strengths, and great work and high levels of productivity will come naturally without any resistance or friction.

"I am terrible at 99% of the things I do. But I work harder than anyone else at the 1% I am good at and that's why I am a millionaire."

-Gary Vaynerchuk

7. Deep Learning (Leveraging Other People's Knowledge)

> *"Ignorant men raise questions that wise men answered a thousand years ago."*
>
> -Johann Wolfgang von Goethe

Leading = reading.

It is no coincidence that so many of the greatest leaders of all time read and studied on a regular (and extensive) basis. But reading isn't the only way to learn. Our knowledge and our mindset is a combination of the:

Books we read

People we spend time with and learn from

Audio we listen to (podcasts, audiobooks, music)

Videos we watch (documentaries, movies, YouTube, television)

Be very precise and ultra-careful about what you take into your mind and who you spend your time with. It shapes who you are.

Invest Your Time Wisely

If you want to get to the top, you must study, model, and learn from the best of the best. Your time is valuable. Don't just spend it studying the good (or even the great). Invest your time studying *the elite*. Here are some famous examples of world-class performers studying the all-time greats who came before them:

Kobe Bryant studied Michael Jordan

Jeff Bezos studied Sam Walton

Brad Stevens (NBA coach) studied John Wooden

Urban Meyer studied Bill Walsh

Mark Zuckerberg studied Bill Gates

Ryan Holiday studied Robert Greene

Mike Tyson studied Alexander the Great

Abraham Lincoln studied George Washington

Franklin Delano Roosevelt studied Theodore Roosevelt

Muhammad Ali studied Sugar Ray Robinson

Dan Kennedy, one of the most brilliant business minds of all time and author of "No B.S. Time Management", on the power of association:

"The phrase "time management" is inaccurate shorthand. You can only manage things that affect your ability to convert time to value, like environment, access, and all the other things discussed in this book.

One of the most significant, that you can control to a great extent, is association—your choices of whom you permit into your world, whom you give time to or invest time with, and whom you look to for ideas, information, and education.

Each minute of your time is made more or less valuable by the condition of your mind, and it is constantly being conditioned by association."

Reading and learning about leadership and maximizing your time is one of the best personal development investments you can ever make.

I estimate that only around 1% of the population has read five outstanding books on leadership and five outstanding books on time mastery. If you take the time to do so and apply the three to five key lessons from each book, you will have a tremendous competitive advantage in leadership and life.

Go to Mount Rushmore

The best study the best. Success leaves clues. Go to the "Mt. Rushmore" of your craft and study, model, and mimic the best practices of the greatest of all time at what you do. It is a powerful "shortcut" to world-class achievement that few will ever use. But those who do, give themselves a tremendous competitive advantage in their field.

This doesn't mean you copy exactly what those on your Mt. Rushmore do. You have your own unique talents and life experiences to bring to the table. But you can learn from and apply the "best practices" of the all-time greats in your field.

A sample framework you can use in your study: 90% of your study time is spent learning about those on the Mt. Rushmore of your craft, 5% spent studying other greats from your field, and 5% spent studying the Mt Rushmore from other fields.

Examples of potential Mt. Rushmore's from different disciplines:

Sports Coaches

-John Wooden

-Nick Saban

-Phil Jackson

-Bill Walsh

U.S. Presidents

-Abraham Lincoln

-George Washington

-Thomas Jefferson

-Theodore Roosevelt

Military Generals

-George Patton

-James Mattis

-Alexander the Great

-Napoleon Bonaparte

Business

-John D. Rockefeller

-Jeff Bezos

-Bill Gates

-Sam Walton

Businesses

-Amazon

-Walmart

-Microsoft

-McDonald's

Inventors

-Nikola Tesla

-Thomas Edison

-Leonardo Di Vinci

-Benjamin Franklin

Athletes

-Michael Jordan

-Kobe Bryant

-Tom Brady

-Michael Phelps

When you study what the best of the best spend their time and energy on, an additional benefit is that you will quickly figure out exactly what NOT to waste your time on. This is wisdom. It can save you years (or decades) of wasted time.

Maximize your study and execution time by going to the Mt. Rushmore of your field. It is one of the best things you can ever do to accelerate your success.

Summary

The "Beat the Clock" Seven-Step Time Mastery system encompasses the mindsets and habits of the people who get the most done on the planet:

1. Maximize Your Energy

"There are three keys to being fully charged each day: doing work that provides meaning to your life, having positive social interactions with others, and taking care of yourself so you have the energy you need to do the first two things."

-Tom Rath

In order to maximize your time, you must maximize your energy.

How to maximize your energy:

Eat foods that give you energy (that you also enjoy), and avoid foods that make you tired or give you "brain fog"

Get good quality sleep

Do exercise that you enjoy with people you like

Drink plenty of water

Spend time with energizing people

2. The Power of One (The 80/20 Principle)

"Productivity can be boiled down to one word—FOCUS."

-Mel Robbins

Have ONE key, measurable, non-negotiable, high-impact goal.

Do the ONE most important, highest-impact task every day to get you closer to achieving that goal.

Spend at least half of your workday on the ONE TASK that has the biggest impact on achieving your NUMBER ONE most important goal.

3. Say "NO" to Almost Everything

"If you never did 75% of what you do every day,
it wouldn't matter."

-Dan Peña

Be incredibly lazy at the things that don't matter and incredibly disciplined at the things that do.

Practice "The Power of No". The happiest and most successful people say "NO" the most, and are continuously simplifying everything in their life and work.

4. Extreme Time-Blocking

> "You will need to put up barriers to protect your time so you can serve more people."

> -Russell Brunson

Extreme time-blocking is one of the ultimate secrets of productivity.

Forget "to-do lists". They are overwhelming and stressful.

Instead, schedule all of the important things you do into your daily calendar on your phone (or a physical daily planner if you prefer). Write out your day, scheduling all activities and time-blocking everything.

We must work from a calendar, not a to-do list.

5. Live Faster (Parkinson's Law)

> "Success loves speed. Delay kills dreams."

> -Craig Ballantyne

Having a healthy sense of urgency is one of the greatest competitive advantages in business (and life).

Focusing on being 10% more productive each day gives you over a FULL MONTH of extra productivity a year.

Parkinson's Law: "Work expands so as to fill the time available for its completion". The amount of time that one has to perform a task is the amount of time it will take to complete the task.

6. Work in Your 1-2 Strengths (Ikigai)

"Working on your weaknesses is a huge flaw. Get great at what you're good at. We only need to be good at one or two things and we can make an impact on the world."

-Dean Graziosi

Working in the areas of your one or two biggest strengths is one of the most useful productivity tools imaginable.

You will be happier and more successful when you work in the areas of your natural strengths. You'll get more done in less time because you are naturally good at it. You'll get more joy out of the work you do because you are naturally inclined to it.

7. Deep Learning (Leveraging Other People's Knowledge)

"Ignorant men raise questions that wise men answered a thousand years ago."

-Johann Wolfgang von Goethe

Leading = reading.

It is no coincidence that so many of the greatest leaders of all time read and studied on a regular (and extensive) basis. But reading isn't the only way to learn. Our knowledge and our mindset is a combination of the:

Books we read

People we spend time with and learn from

Audio we listen to (podcasts, audiobooks, music)

Videos we watch (documentaries, movies, YouTube, television)

Be very precise and ultra-careful about what you take into your mind and who you spend your time with. It shapes who you are.

Outstanding Time Mastery Books

15 Secrets Successful People Know About Time Management by Kevin Kruse

The 150 Most Effective Ways to Boost Your Energy by Jonny Bowden

No B.S. Time Management by Dan Kennedy

One Thing by Gary Keller

Essentialism by Greg McKeown

Don't overthink this.

It's not that complicated.

Make it a habit to read for just 15 minutes a day.

You will never regret it.

> "Anyone who stops learning is old, whether twenty or eighty. Anyone who keeps learning stays young."
>
> -Henry Ford

Time Mastery Power Questions

What if I could only subtract to solve problems? What should I put on my not-to-do list?   -Tim Ferriss

Instead of asking, "how can I do this?", ask "how can this get done?".   -Kevin Kruse

Will it make the boat go faster? The UK rowing team is going to the Olympics. There was no way they were going to win. The coach says, "Here's what we're going to do: for the next 18 months, every single decision we make, we are going to ask ourselves, "Will it make the boat go faster?". Hey guys, let's go for ice cream. Will it make the boat go faster? No. We're not having ice cream. Hey guys, let's go hang out with the girls. Will it make the boat go faster? No. The only things they did were things that made the boat go faster." Probably very boring, probably very painful. They won the gold. It's no different in life. Maximize your time.   Joe De Sena

How much would I pay to get this day back when I am 70? How much would I pay to get this time back, to go back in time when I am 70? How much would I pay to go back and not waste those days?   Alex Becker

If I had a gun against my head and can only work for two hours a week, what would I do?   Tim Ferriss

What's the one thing I could do every single day, that a year from now, would totally change my life?   Aaron Doughty

If you are ever at the crossroads of making a difficult decision, always ask yourself, "What is the hard choice?". Then take that path.   Jerzy Gregorek

We always WIN (What's Important Now?).   Larry Gelwix, Highland high school rugby coach with 20 state championships and a record of 418 wins and 10 losses over 36 years

What would this look like if it were easy?   Tim Ferriss

Do you really think millionaires and billionaires walk around with a to-do list? Do you really think Bill Gates, Donald Trump, and Warren Buffett write a long to-do list and prioritize items as A1, A2, B1, B2, C1, and on and on? Do you really think Steve Jobs kept a to-do list and asked himself several times a day, "What's my next action?"   -Kevin Kruse, 15 Secrets Successful People Know About Time Management

Every day, ask yourself, "Who did I help today?" This will give you a better life.   James Altucher

If you have a ten-year plan to get somewhere, why can't you get there in six months?   Peter Thiel

What is the one thing I can do such that by doing it everything else will become easier or necessary?   Gary Keller

Meeting Mastery

1. Brief. You can hold effective meetings for large organizations in as quick as 15 minutes. Only invite people who are necessary. Meetings of more than eight people have a "point of diminishing returns" in terms of productivity. Productivity fact: small teams working on a problem or innovation get more done. Jeff Bezos's "two pizza rule" at Amazon: Never have a meeting where two pizzas couldn't feed the entire group.

2. Bright. Positive and solution-oriented. Start and end the meeting on a positive note. This can be starting the meeting with what people did over the weekend, gratitude, positive things happening in the organization, positive performance by team members, and ending the meeting with clear action steps. If people absolutely need to vent or get things off of their chest, limit it to the first five to ten minutes of the meeting.

3.   Future-focused.   Ideas and solutions.   No endless "archeological digs" into the past. Avoid talking about or complaining   about   past   occurrences,   past   employees, etc. These things are now in the past. A great meeting is about today and the future.

4. Clear start times and end times. Start on time and end on time.   Team   members   and   leaders   should   not   be late. Meetings should end on time. 10% of the time or less, the organization will be facing a challenge so large or pressing that you need to go over the allotted time. In my experience, most meetings should be an hour or less. 90 minutes maximum. As a leader, you will notice that you will begin to lose people's attention around the 55-minute mark, and anything over 90 minutes will be mentally (and sometimes emotionally) draining for your team.   Brilliant advice from time management expert, Kevin Kruse: "Start meetings exactly on time and end them five minutes earlier than scheduled."

5. Clear agenda of five discussion items or less, starting the meeting with the number one most important topic of discussion.

6. The best meetings have strong "moderators" leading them, keeping everyone focused and moving. Parkinson's Law of Triviality: Most organizations and people will spend the most time on trivial issues and the least time on important issues. A strong moderator will cut off long-winded stories, tangents, and off-topic discussions.

7. Get closure on one topic before going to the next. If you can't make a decision on a topic or are becoming bored with the topic, either table it for the next meeting or make a decision now.

8. Avoid all cell phone or laptop usage unless it's absolutely to take notes or to look something up. No text messaging or answering calls; it's distracting and also inefficient because it's multitasking.

9. Clear action steps at the end of the meeting, with specific individuals who will do the work, and also clear deadlines. 3D Method: Make a Decision and stick to it. Delegate the task to someone. Set a Deadline.

10. Figure out your best meeting cadence for your organization. For example: Five-minute daily team huddles, 15-minute weekly meetings, 55-minute monthly meetings, 90-minute quarterly meetings, one-day yearly meetings.

8. Talent Mastery: Success Is In The Setup

> *"We hire people who want to create the best things in the world."*
>
> *-Steve Jobs*

The best leaders attract, develop, and keep the best talent in their market and field. Period.

In any organization on the planet, 95% of your success is in "The Setup".

What is "The Setup"?

1. Create a big, energizing "Heroic Mission" that inspires and pulls the entire organization and its people towards it.

2. Do everything you can to attract, develop, and keep the best talent in your market and field who are deeply inspired and energized by your organization's specific Heroic Mission.

Don't overthink this.

It's not that complicated.

You are not just hiring. You are selecting true believers in your big energizing Heroic Mission.

Big Energizing Heroic Mission

> *"If you have a problem hiring in this market, it's because your culture is not attracting talent to come and work for you."*
>
> *-Donald Burns*

The best cultures on the planet have big energizing Heroic Missions.

Examples:

Be the best in the market, country, or world at what you do.

Win a major award for your organization.

Create a major breakthrough in your field (science and technology).

Great service to humanity and the world.

Win a major championship for your team (sports).

Defend and protect your nation (military).

Think different. Think bigger. If you want to attract the best talent in your field, you've got to give them a big energizing Heroic Mission to get excited about.

Best Talent (Success is in the Setup Hiring)

> *"If I meet with someone and they don't have energy, if they can't energize with their passion, the meeting is over in 90 seconds. Energy is the #1 thing I look for."*
>
> *-Dan Peña*

Over the last 20 years, these are the three traits I have observed in the best team members in any organization:

1. High Warmth

2. High Standards

3. Energizer

Here's a simple breakdown of each.

1. High Warmth

Individuals with high warmth are lifters. They smile easily and they laugh often. They are quick to compliment or help a team member in need. They are warm and welcoming to new team members. *They prioritize giving over taking.*

2. High Standards

They are committed to excellence in everything they do—inside and outside of work. They are always looking to improve. They don't do the bare minimum, but continuously look to do "a little extra". They are self-motivated. Winners keep winning. *The best predictor of future performance is past performance.*

3. Energizer

They are enthusiastic and energized by the work and vision of the organization. This allows them to energize others and also have the stamina to do the sometimes long and extra work required to get closer to achieving the big vision. They are confident and optimistic in themselves and others. They avoid being "mindlessly negative" and draining the energy of those around them. *They have a "fire and a spark" that lights up a room.*

In order to attract new team members with these three traits, you must ask yourself:

1. Do I live these three traits as a leader?

2. Do our current team members in the organization live these traits?

Current Team Member and Leadership Diagnostic

Here's a quick four-question diagnostic test. It's a deeper look at your team members and the culture they create. Ask yourself these questions about all of your current leadership and team members:

1. If they weren't currently part of our organization, *would I hire them again?*

2. Do they bring *joy or growth* to their fellow team members? (High Warmth)

3. Are they *continuously improvement-minded and relentlessly solution-focused*? (High Standards)

4. Are they *passionate and energized* by the work and vision? (Energy)

If the answer is no to any of these questions, it is paramount that you address that team member or leader as soon as possible. They are negatively affecting the ability of your organization to attract and keep the best talent in your market or field. Begin by asking them questions, then coach to help them become the best they can be.

The Ten Best Observable Traits

"When interviewing a job candidate, ask yourself: How would I feel if this person were working for the competition?"

-Jim Sullivan

The following are the most important observable traits I've seen in job interviews. This list was derived from personally conducting hundreds of interviews, as well as helping many organizations interview potential candidates or promote team members to leadership positions. Here are ten observable traits that show energy, warmth, and confidence.

1. Shows up at least FIVE TO TEN MINUTES EARLY for the interview, the earlier the better.

2. Well DRESSED and well GROOMED.

3. Energizing presence (listen to your gut).

4. SMILES easily and often during the interview.

5. Confident and open BODY LANGUAGE.

6. Interviewee ASKS YOU questions (shows confidence).

7. Looks you in the eye when talking and listening (good EYE CONTACT).

8. Shows the appropriate level of RESPECT for the conversation.

9. Has GOOD MANNERS. Extremely polite.

10. Do they respond to the questions with ENERGY and ENTHUSIASM?

BONUS: At ease with small talk and CASUAL CONVERSATION.

Inversion

Inversion = know exactly what you are NOT looking for.

It is just as important to know exactly what traits you are *looking to avoid* in a potential hire.

Here are the *opposite traits* of our key three traits of High Warmth, High Standard, and Energy:

1. Low warmth. Doesn't smile easily. This can be caused by nervousness, so try to "loosen up" the interview if necessary.

2. Unprepared. Doesn't know anything about your organization. Late to the interview with no explanation. Underdressed.

3. Low Energy. Doesn't answer questions with enthusiasm. Doesn't seem excited about the work and/or the opportunity to work for your organization.

Expert interviewers are constantly looking for red flags. These are reasons NOT to hire the candidate.

You don't become great at interviewing and talent acquisition until you start interviewing candidates and NOT hiring some of them. But ALWAYS let a candidate who you do not hire keep their dignity.

As a leader, you must make sure that the candidate is not only a great fit for your organization, but that your organization is a *great fit for them.*

Effective Interview Questions

The following questions were collected and compiled over the last 20 years. They are some of my personal favorites, and have been categorized into our High Standards, High Warmth, and Energy traits. I have found them ultra-useful in identifying great hires.

1. High Standards Questions

Why do you want to work at _____? (They did do their research and homework on your organization)

How old were you when you got your first job? (The younger the better, as this shows work ethic at an early age)

What are your three proudest accomplishments in life so far?

Tell me what you were like in high school? Sports, academics, school activities, friendships, awards or championships, etc.

Please describe yourself in three words.

Where do you see yourself ideally in five years?

How do you feel about being on time?

What have you learned over the last year (outside of school)? (This indicates a learning mindset)

How have you improved yourself over the last year? (This indicates a growth mindset)

What one non-fiction book had the biggest positive impact on your life? (This indicates a learning and growth mindset)

Did you have any leadership roles at a young age? Tell me about those (or any) leadership roles you have had in the past. (Leadership roles at a young age such as high school is a tremendous indicator of leadership potential)

What three qualities do you think are necessary to be a great leader?

What are your three most important work-related values?

Please provide an example of a situation where you demonstrated each value at work.

What team sports have you played in your life (or group activities you've participated in such as music, Boy Scouts/Girl Scouts, etc.) from elementary school up to the present? (Participation in group activities indicates potential to successfully operate in a team environment)

When you think of the word "successful", who are the first three people that come to mind and why?

Why are you better than the other people we have interviewed? (Confidence test)

Everyone thinks (their name) is great, but... Interview question by General Stanley McChrystal to find out how self-aware they are about the perception others have of you. The most important thing is not their specific answer, but that they have an answer.

Do you respect yourself? Everyone is going to say yes. Ask them to give you examples of how they respect themselves. Look for ways that they actually go out of their way to respect themselves. Examples: I take care of myself, I work out, I eat right, I work hard, I set strong boundaries in my relationships, I make sure my kids are in bed by a certain time so I can have some time with my spouse, etc. (Favorite Interview question of Donald Burns, restaurant expert)

Two-stage interview: Ask them to read a book between interviews, then quiz them on a few chapters (this will weed people out who are not serious).

2. High Warmth Questions

Do you consider yourself a giver? Please explain/give examples.

What charitable or volunteer activities have you participated in within the last year?

3. High Warmth and High Standards Questions

Who are your three biggest heroes? Why?

If you could have dinner with any three people, alive or passed on, who would they be and why?

Why did you leave your last job? And the one before that? (Manager of the Century Jack Welch question)

What three people had the biggest positive impact on you and why?

What are your hobbies?

Ask for the three things the person liked least about his or her last (or current) company. (IMPORTANT)

What books or movies had the biggest impact on you?

How would your previous co-workers describe you in three words?

What will your job references say about you when I call them?

4. Energy Questions

What would you like to talk about? (What energizes them?)

What are three things that upset you/try your patience?

How would your friends describe you in three words?

Summary

Become the type of leader that attracts and keeps the best talent in your market and field.

In any organization on the planet, 95% of your success is in "The Setup".

What is The Setup?

1. Create a big, energizing "Heroic Mission" that inspires and pulls the entire organization and its people towards it.

2. Do everything you can to attract, develop, and keep the best talent in your market and field who are deeply inspired and energized by your organization's specific Heroic Mission.

Don't overthink this.

It's not that complicated.

Over the last 20 years, these are the three traits I have observed in the best team members in any organization:

1. High Warmth

2. High Standards

3. Energizer

Here's a quick four-question diagnostic test. It's a deeper look at your team members and the culture they create. Ask yourself these questions about all of your current leadership and team members:

1. If they weren't currently part of our organization, *would I hire them again?*

2. Do they bring *joy or growth* to their fellow team members? (High Warmth)

3. Are they *continuously improvement-minded and relentlessly solution-focused*? (High Standards)

4. Are they *passionate and energized* by the work and vision? (Energy)

If the answer is no to any of these questions, it is paramount that you address that team member or leader as soon as possible. They are negatively affecting the ability of your organization to attract and keep the best talent in your market or field. Begin by asking them questions, then coach to help them become the best they can be.

Inversion = know exactly what you are NOT looking for.

Here are the opposite traits of our key three traits of high warmth, high standards, and energy:

1. Low Warmth

2. Unprepared

3. Low Energy

Expert interviewers are constantly looking for red flags. These are reasons NOT to hire the candidate.

Don't overthink this.

It's not that complicated.

9. Culture Mastery: Cultural Architecture and Engineering

> *"Slogans and vision statements on a wall don't work. Belief systems work. Culture works."*
>
> *-Horst Schulze*

The most successful (and happiest) organizational cultures on the planet all have three simple fundamentals that create the foundation for world-class performance:

1. A Heroic Mission. The vision/mission is so big, bold, and inspiring that it pulls the whole team and organization towards it. *It is a clear aiming point for everyone.*

2. High Warmth. Team members are treated, and treat each other, with *care, respect, and dignity*.

3. High Standards. Standards of performance (and attitude) are much higher than other organizations in their market and field. *The best organizations have ELITE standards.*

Heroic Mission.

High Warmth.

High Standards.

The Ten-Second Culture Test

How to Observe an Organization and Tell if it Has a Great Culture in Ten Seconds or Less:

1. Movement with purpose. Not frantic, stressed movement. Calm, deliberate, and continuous movement. The organization looks like a busy, productive beehive. High Standards.

2. Smiles and laughter. Customers and fellow team members are greeted with smiles. Laughter between teammates. High Warmth.

3. The newest team member knows the One-Sentence Mission Statement.

Here are some examples of organizations that have a Heroic Mission, High Warmth, and High Standards:

Clemson Football

San Antonio Spurs Basketball

Minnesota Gophers Football

Google

Texas Roadhouse

Chick-Fil-A

Wegmans grocery stores

Trader Joe's

Three Powerful Culture Questions

Here are three simple questions that, if asked on a regular basis, will build a best-in-class organization:

1. What's it gonna take to be the best?

2. Why would the best talent in our market and field want to work here?

3. What can destroy our culture (or organization), and how do we avoid it?

Don't overthink this.

It's not that complicated.

We can break down each powerful question into what the answers may be for your organization.

1. What's it gonna take to be the best?

A heroic mission

High standards

High warmth

Relentless solution focus

Continuous improvement mindset

Sense of urgency

Best talent

Best leadership

2. Why would the best talent in our market and field want to work here?

Competent and caring leadership who they respect, admire, and can learn from

Surrounded by other great, talented, and caring teammates

An inspiring and energizing mission

Growth opportunities in knowledge (or position) within the organization

Fair compensation (within 10% above or below market average)

3. What can destroy our culture (or organization), and how do we avoid it?

Poor leadership/management

Negative and/or low-performing team members

No clear mission and direction

No clear standards of performance and driving core values

World-class Culture Architecture and Engineering System

"A great culture is pretty simple. Don't just have good players. Have good people."
-Steve Kerr, 8x NBA champion and head coach of the Golden State Warriors

The following is the "World-Class Culture Architecture and Engineering" 90-Day Plan.

Yes, a world-class culture can be established in 90 days or less.

This seven-step process can be used by organizations of two team members, all the way up to two million.

The seven steps are divided into "Three Pillars":

1. Inversion. Figure out exactly what the *biggest team member and leadership de-motivators* are and address them quickly.

2. Guidance System. Create a guidance system of a clear mission and vision, core values, and standards. This Guidance System should be: 1) So short that it can be written on a napkin, and 2) So simple that it can be understood by a twelve-year-old. The Guidance Systems of some of the most successful businesses and organizations on the planet fit these two criteria. *Short and simple is memorable and easy to implement.* Long and complicated is forgettable and difficult to execute with consistency.

3. Success is in the Setup. This is talent acquisition and leadership development. The goal is to attract and keep the best talent in your market and industry through having *the best leadership in your market and industry*.

We'll now break down each of the Three Pillars.

Pillar #1: Inversion

Step One: Data, Data, Data

> *"Strive to make your team's job easier by listening to them."*
> *-Verne Harnish, Scaling Up*

As a leader, you must continuously listen to the thoughts and feelings of your team members. You must pay attention to the "emotional temperature" of your organization.

You must know what makes your people happy, frustrated, excited, and angry.

Here are some of the most effective ways to be an "Expert Listener":

1. One-on-one conversations (best)

2. Anonymous surveys (best)

3. Managing by walking around

4. Leadership/management meetings

5. Team member focus groups

6. Suggestion boxes

7. Easy accessibility to the president/CEO/head coach for team members (by phone, email, in-person conversations, etc.)

Anonymous Team Member Surveys

> *"In real estate, the main mantra is "location, location, location"; in building a quality work environment, it is "communication, communication, communication."*
>
> *-Bill Cottringer, PhD*

A tool I use in every organization I work with is *anonymous team member and management surveys.*

When they are anonymous, they allow people to speak freely about what is really going on in the trenches and front lines of your organization.

A simple four-question survey you can implement today:

1. On a scale of 1-10, how likely are you to recommend working for your leadership to someone you know?

2. What are three things you like about working for our organization? What are your three favorite things about the job?

3. What are three specific things we can do to improve your work experience?

4. If you were the owner/CEO/President/head coach for a week, what would you do to improve the organization?

Bonus questions:

5. What are some ways our organization can reduce costs and save money today?

6. What are some ways our organization can grow and add more customers?

Two crucial things you MUST do when implementing anonymous team member surveys:

1. Over-communicate that the surveys are *100% anonymous*. People must feel safe enough to express their true thoughts and feelings.

2. Create and begin to implement a solution to address and *remedy at least one of the top concerns within 72 hours* of the entire team completing the surveys. There is almost always a common thread that runs through a large number of the surveys. Choose something that you can remedy quickly and easily and do it within 72 hours. This shows your people that you take their concerns seriously.

The number one mistake I see organizations make with anonymous surveys is that they conduct the surveys...then do nothing with the results.

This is a slap in the face to team members. They took the time to share their thoughts, and their leadership did nothing.

Those leaders would have been better off never asking for their team member's thoughts and feelings in the first place. Instead, they wasted everyone's time, created distrust, and lost respect.

Don't be that leader.

Listen, learn, and make positive changes.

Don't overthink this.

It's not that complicated.

Step Two: Don't De-Motivate

> *"How do you hire extraordinary people? The answer is, they already work for you. You just haven't given them a pathway."*
>
> *-Daniel Burris*

Address any de-motivators uncovered by your conversations and anonymous surveys.

The most common de-motivators in any organization are as follows (in order of the biggest impact):

1. Poor leadership and management. This is far and above the biggest de-motivator in any organization.

2. Poor teammate performance or attitude.

3. Lack of vision, mission, goals, and/or overall direction of the organization.

Address any leadership and/or team members who are not living the highest standards of attitude and/or performance.

Your lowest-performing leaders and team members set the acceptable levels in your organization

Do an 80/20 analysis and address individuals in order of magnitude of the lowest performance or poorest attitude. Start by asking them questions about their performance or attitude, and *believe in them* that they can improve it.

Apply coaching and training if necessary. If they refuse to change after the appropriate amounts of caring conversations and coaching, it may be time to part ways with them.

Addressing the biggest de-motivators in your organization can have a huge positive impact on your organizational performance and the happiness and success of your people.

"Customer service isn't just for those who face the public. It also extends to people inside an organization who deal with each other."

-Horst Schulze

Pillar #2: Guidance System

Step Three: A Heroic Mission

"Purpose is the new competitive advantage."
-Caroline Castrillon

Create a one-sentence "World-class Why" mission statement. It serves as your clear aiming point.

World-class Why missions:

1) Become the best-in-class,

2) The pursuit of excellence,

3) Great service to the world.

Your World-class Why drives every decision in your organization.

You can ask yourself in any situation:

Does this get me closer to achieving the mission or farther away?

Everything you do is a binary, yes or no answer to this question.

> *"Understand your why. It all starts here. Without a strong why, you'll soon be back in your old habits again. As soon as you face even the slightest bit of headwind, you'll be eager to return to the path of least resistance. Not so when you have a great why."*
>
> *-Dean Graziosi*

A World-class Why gives elite achievers and organizations the stamina to keep moving forward, despite the adversity and pain required to walk among the best performers on the planet.

A World-class Why is a tremendously powerful and effective way to lead an organization to best-in-class performance and team member happiness. This type of Why is commonly referred to as a "Mission Statement".

A World-class Why "Mission Statement" for an organization is:

A Bold Heroic Mission That Creates Visionary Work

A Quest to Solve a Giant Problem or Create Something on an Enormous Scale

There are only three World-class Why's:

1. Become the Best in the World (Compete)

2. The Pursuit of Excellence (Healthy Obsession)

3. Positive Impact (Service to Others and the World)

Some world-class achievers and organizations have only one of the three as their World-class Why.

Others have two, or all three of the Why's driving their success.

In my estimation:

1 in 100 organizations have one "World-class Why Heroic Mission" clearly driving all members of their organization on a daily basis

1 in 500 have two World-class Why's

1 in 1000 have all three

> "The book Corporate Culture and Performance supports the idea that purpose leads to profit. The authors, Harvard professors John Kotter and James Heskett, showed that over ten years, purpose-led companies outperformed their counterparts in stock price by a factor of twelve."
>
> -Caroline Castrillon

Examples of World-class Why one-sentence mission statements from individual leaders:

Colonize Mars and save humanity (Elon Musk and SpaceX)

Win an NBA championship (Michael Jordan)

Put a man on the moon (John F. Kennedy)

Win the Super Bowl (Tom Brady)

End segregation (Dr. Martin Luther King)

All of these incredible achievements can be summed up by a one-sentence mission statement.

Don't overthink this.

It's not that complicated.

Organizational Heroic Mission Statements

Three "World-class Why" Options for Your "Big Energizing Mission"

1. Best-in-Class/Award-Winning

2. The Pursuit of Excellence

3. Service and Positive Impact on Others

1. Best-in-Class/Award-Winning examples:

American Express: We work hard every day to make American Express the world's most respected service brand.

Amazon: To be Earth's most customer-centric company, where customers can find and discover anything they might want to buy online, and endeavors to offer its customers the lowest possible prices.

PayPal: To build the web's most convenient, secure, cost-effective payment solution.

2. Pursuit of Excellence

Nordstrom: To give customers the most compelling shopping experience possible.

Google: To organize the world's information and make it universally accessible and useful.

Southwest Airlines: Dedication to the highest quality of Customer Service delivered with a sense of warmth, friendliness, individual pride, and Company Spirit.

Universal Health Services, Inc.: To provide superior quality healthcare services that: PATIENTS recommend to family and friends, PHYSICIANS prefer for their patients, PURCHASERS select for their clients, EMPLOYEES are proud of, and INVESTORS seek for long-term returns.

3. Service and Positive Impact on Others

Nike: Bring inspiration and innovation to every athlete in the world.

Tesla: To accelerate the world's transition to sustainable energy.

American Red Cross: To prevent and alleviate human suffering in the face of emergencies by mobilizing the power of volunteers and the generosity of donors.

Walmart: We save people money so they can live better.

IKEA: To create a better everyday life for the many people.

Step Four: Highest Standards of Performance

> *"Our whole purpose of owning a business comes down to one thing: protecting standards."*
>
> *-Jon Taffer*

Make a list of the one to fifteen most important, non-negotiable team member standards.

Focus on the top-three highest-impact first, and over-communicate those three specifically for 90 days.

Standards are the daily habits, behaviors, and standard operating procedures of your organization.

Having clearly-defined High Standards does not make it harder on your people, it actually makes it easier because:

1. Everyone knows what is expected of them and there is no confusion

2. Everyone knows where they stand in terms of performance

3. Things run smoother when there are higher standards

4. Better results and progress lead to more team member happiness and confidence

Here is a list of what I call "Platinum Standards". Most of them can be applied to the vast majority of organizations, regardless of the industry:

1. Treat Each Other Well (Most Important, All the Next Standards Support This One)

2. Safety First

3. Show Up on Time

4. Locked in Focus (No Cell Phone Use Without Permission, And Never in Front of a Customer/Guest/Client)

5. Three is a Crowd (Congregating with More Than Two Team Members in Front of a Customer/Guest/Client is Not Warm, Welcoming, or Professional)

6. Ladies and Gentlemen (Dress and Speak Professionally)

7. Be Warm and Welcoming

8. Have a Sense of Urgency

9. Say "Yes" and "Thank You" at Every Opportunity

10. Keep Your Word (Do What You Say You Are Going to Do)

11. Do a Little Extra

12. 100% Guest/Client/Customer Happiness Guarantee (Never Argue with Someone, Make it Right When Things Go Wrong)

13. Tell the Truth Faster (Be Respectfully Honest and Open With Each Other)

14. Act with Integrity (No Lying, No Stealing, No Alcohol or Drug Use)

15. Be Useful (To Each Other)

16. Use Good Judgement Always

> *"Be tough on standards, easy on people. We put our people first—in turn, our associates stay for 5, 10, 15, 20, even 25 years as proven by extremely low turnover rates, which are consistently well below national restaurant averages. We always prioritize culture over profit, and yet, our bottom line is higher than that of comparable companies."*
>
> *-Cameron Mitchell, restaurateur*

Once your simple organizational High Standards are set, they must be:

1. Over-communicated from day one (clearly covered and explained on a new hire's very first day).

2. Exemplified by leadership in their own daily habits and behaviors.

3. Upheld by leadership, from the newest team member all the way up to the one with the longest tenure.

Over-communicate and exemplify your standards.

What you permit is what you promote. You must hold everyone accountable.

Don't overthink this.

Just do it.

Step Five: High Warmth (Elite Core Values)

"Mantras are like a North Star. This is who we are, this is what we do. Constantly living it. The best cultures have a "mantra map", a handful of sayings and symbols that make sense for them and that they broadcast. It is "emotional GPS"."

-Daniel Coyle, The Culture Code

Your "Elite Core Values" are not who you want to be or aspire to achieve. Your Elite Core Values are who you are today. Day in and day out.

No exceptions.

No excuses.

These Elite Core Values create a "language of success" for the entire organization, starting with leadership. The right ones only work...always.

The right Elite Core Values will create high warmth within your organization, to and from your customers, and outwardly towards the community.

Create one to fifteen Elite Core Values and over-communicate them for 90 days.

Then over-communicate them forever. Your non-negotiable core values must become a way of life within your organization.

They are daily landmarks on your road to best-in-class success.

Address anyone who is not living these Elite Core Values, starting with leadership.

The right Elite Core Values will guide every organizational decision:

Who you hire

Who you part ways with

Who you promote

Who you reward (bonuses)

Who you give leadership positions to

How you make decisions (large and small)

Your Elite Core Values should be short, punchy, and memorable. They should be unique. They should not be long, boring, and generic. They should have "heart and soul".

They will serve as daily "mantras" and become the foundation of your organizational culture.

The Six Core Values of Elite Performance

The following are the six Elite Core Values I use to help turn around struggling organizations. They also work equally well for thriving organizations that are looking to level-up and become best-in-class.

1. Lock in (Focus on What is Most Important)

2. Bring the Juice (Positive Energy)

3. Turn Up the Love (Be Kind, Be Useful, and Reduce the Stress of Others)

4. Be Brilliant at the Basics (Fundamentals, Fundamentals, Fundamentals)

5. Nobody Notices Normal (Show Up Different)

6. 1% Better Than Yesterday (Continuous Improvement Mindset)

These six Elite Core Values will create high-level success at any time, anywhere, in any organization on the planet.

The legendary company, Zappos, use these ten simple core values to create a multi-billion-dollar business with a cult-like following:

1. Deliver WOW Through Service

2. Embrace and Drive Change

3. Create Fun and a Little Weirdness

4. Be Adventurous, Creative, and Open-Minded

5. Pursue Growth and Learning

6. Build Open and Honest Relationships with Communication

7. Build a Positive Team and Family Spirit

8. Do More with Less

9. Be Passionate and Determined

10. Be Humble

Brilliantly short. Beautifully simple. And memorable. Don't overthink this. Keep it simple.

The following are examples of "Memorable vs. Forgettable Core Values".

Forgettable: Work hard

Memorable: All day, every day.

Forgettable: Focus

Memorable: Focus on the few, not the many.

Tony Hsieh, billionaire founder of Zappos, on core values:

"In his book "Good to Great", Jim Collins researched what separated the good companies from the great ones in terms of long-term financial performance.

The great ones had two important ingredients that separated them from the good ones.

One of them was that they all had strong cultures. We formalized the definition of our culture into our ten core values."

Your Elite Core Values MUST be over-communicated. They cannot be the "flavor of the week", where they are rolled out once with great enthusiasm, then completely forgotten. They must become part of your company's DNA.

They must be upheld like the Ten Commandments or the U.S. Constitution.

They are the laws of the land, and your team members, customers, and community will be better off because you follow them.

> *"Repetition is vital. For example, let's say that you've told your employees that "customer focus is vital to the company's continued success". You have to repeat it in every conversation with employees, every speech, and every written statement. Bright people often think that if they've said it once, the point has been made. No, the point needs to be repeated."*
>
> *-Bill Conerly*

Elite Core Values Examples

The Ten Common Themes of Elite Core Values:

1. Morality/ethics

2. Commitment to excellence

3. Treating each other well

4. Extreme customer focus

5. Frugality

6. Thinking bigger

7. Thinking different

8. Speed/sense of urgency

9. Narrow focus

10. Continuous improvement

Elite Core Value examples from eight organizations who consistently perform at a world-class level:

Zappos: Deliver WOW through service

Zappos: Create fun and a little weirdness

Zappos: Do more with less

Zappos: Be humble

Google: Focus on the user and all else will follow

Google: It's best to do one thing really, really well

Google: Fast is better than slow

Google: You can make money without doing evil

Google: Great just isn't good enough

Amazon: Customer obsession

Amazon: Have a backbone, disagree and commit

Amazon: Insist on the highest standards

Amazon: Think big

Walmart: Listen to everyone in your company

Walmart: Control your expenses better than your competition

Walmart: Swim upstream

Tesla and Space X: Move fast

Tesla and Space X: Do the impossible

Tesla and Space X: We are ALL IN

Nike: Master the fundamentals

Nike: Do the right thing

Nike: We are on the offense—always

Apple: Simple, not complex

Apple: Say no

Apple: Accept mistakes

Chick-Fil-A: Personal excellence

Chick-Fil-A: Continuous improvement

Pillar #3: Success is in the Setup

Step Six: Best Leadership

> *"So goes the leader, so goes the culture. So goes the culture, so goes the company."*
>
> *-Simon Sinek*

The number-one most important factor of establishing and perpetuating a world-class culture is the leadership of the organization. No exceptions. Without leadership who live and uphold the standards and values of the organization, your culture will always be "driving around with its emergency brake on". No exceptions, no excuses, your leadership must be "keepers of your cultural flame".

You must be ultra-careful of who you hire or promote into a leadership position. I have seen bad decisions in this area completely wreck morale, de-motivate great team members, and cripple once great organizations.

Three important things to look for in your leadership candidate:

1. High personal standards inside and outside of work, and the ability to hold team members to high standards.

2. High warmth; caring about the success and happiness of their team members inside and outside of work.

3. Energized by the work and mission of the organization, and the ability to energize team members.

"Morale of an organization is not built from the bottom up; it filters from the top down."

-Peter Kyne

For your current leadership, establish a learning and development program with regular coaching sessions. This can be done by scheduling regular sessions (weekly, bi-weekly, or monthly) with a mentor inside the organization, and/or a reputable leadership coach from outside the organization.

Coaching or mentoring sessions should be done one-on-one. The sessions should be custom-tailored to the unique leadership challenges he or she is facing, as well as working on the specific leadership traits they need to improve on. Leadership development topics for these sessions can include:

How to achieve goals and hit performance metrics

Time management

Confidence building

Best self-education resources

Energizing and inspiring team members

How to challenge team members to do better through one-on-one conversations

How to have difficult conversations

Health and wellness

Stress reduction

Work-life integration

The return on the time and money invested into leadership development cannot be overstated. It is easily one of the best investments an organization can ever make.

> *"To win in the marketplace,*
> *you must first win in the workplace."*
> *-Doug Conant, CEO, 2001–2011,*
> *Campbell Soup Company*

Step Seven: Best Talent

My definition of "Best Talent":

1. Passionate about doing great work in your industry/field

2. Treats others with warmth, respect, and dignity

3. Energized and inspired by the mission of your organization

Here is what best talent is not:

Perceived IQ

Fancy degrees

"Experience" in the field

What that person can "do for you"

Here are the three traits that the Best Talent have, followed by my definition of each:

1. Smarts (High Standards)

Expert listener

Relentless solution focus

Continuous improvement mindset

2. Hearts (High Warmth)

Treat others with respect and dignity

Does things legally, morally, and ethically

True to their word (they do what they say they are going to do)

3. Energy

Energized by the work and mission of the organization

Energizer for others

Strength of personality (confidence)

These are ways that I define Best Talent. You can have your own. What matters is that you have one, and are crystal clear in the traits you are looking for in your team members and leadership. Once you have your definition of Best Talent, you must ask yourself this every day:

Why would the best talent in our market and field want to work here?

Here's a few important reasons why:

Competent and caring leadership who they respect, admire, and can learn from

Surrounded by other Best Talent

An inspiring and clear "World-class Why" big energizing mission

High standards of performance and attitude

Mindless negativity is not tolerated (complaining, venting, blaming, gossiping, condemning)

Growth opportunities in knowledge or position within the organization

Treated with respect and dignity

Valued and appreciated

Fair compensation (within 10% above or below market average)

Don't overthink this.

It's not that complicated.

Don't talk about it.

BE about it.

How to create a culture that attracts, develops, and keeps the best talent in your market and field?

1. Establish the top-three, non-negotiable Best Talent hiring traits of High Warmth (Hearts), High Standards (Smarts), and Energy. Or whatever the top three key traits are for your organization.

2. Address current leadership and team members who are not living your simple Best Talent criteria and your core values.

3. Recognize and reward those who are living and exemplifying your simple Best Talent criteria and your Elite Core Values.

Repeat.

Never stop doing this.

If you stick to this simple formula, you will build and perpetuate a World-class Culture that attracts and keeps the Best Talent in your market and field, who will deliver the best products and services to your customers and community.

Everyone wins.

"You should treat your employees as good, if not better, than your customers."

-Ryan Stewman

Culture Quick Fix

"Building a culture is a three-part process. Believe it. Sell it. Demand it."

-Urban Meyer

If you are looking for a quick fix for a culture that is struggling, here's the three-step process "minimum effective dosage" to get things back on track quickly.

Quick Fix #1: Team member anonymous surveys to see the true state of your organizational morale and happiness (and where specifically you can improve).

Quick Fix #2: Leadership each holds a meaningful, sincere, one-on-one conversation with one team member daily for three months.

No exceptions, no excuses.

The leader must keep the Three Agreement for every conversation:

Show up on time

Keep their word (no last-minute cancellations, outside of an emergency)

Locked in focus (no cell phone or people interruptions during the conversation)

By the leader keeping these Three Agreements, it shows the team member that they are respected and important.

The conversation will have three important parts:

1. Catch the team member doing something right. This is sincere praise for something positive they have done for a teammate, a customer, the organization, or the community.

2. Ask them what the number-one challenge they are facing is. Discuss how they might overcome it. Ask how they think it can be done first, and provide feedback (or other possible solutions if necessary).

3. Cross-examine. Learn something new about your team member. What makes them happy? What makes them frustrated? Where have they been? And where do they want to go?

Be an expert listener.

Be a true believer in that person.

Everyone needs one.

Quick Fix #3: No more mindless negativity (complaining, venting, blaming, gossiping, and condemning as a communication style).

Nature hates a vacuum.

When negativity doesn't exist, that space will inevitably be filled with the opposite:

Positivity

Service to others

Relentless solution focus

Continuous improvement mindset

Over-communicate that mindless negativity is not how we communicate in our organization. Mindless negativity is not good for anyone. By doing everything you can to eliminate it, good things will happen automatically without anyone even trying. Amazing.

There's your "Three-Step Cultural Quick Fix".

Don't overthink it.

Just do it.

Signs of Life: Positive Cultural Growth Metrics

The following are the five things I look for to show us that our cultural architecture and engineering work of High Standards and High Warmth is having a positive effect:

1. Noticeably less mindless negativity

2. Noticeably more smiles and laughter

3. More honest and open communication

4. Performance standards of lower performers and/or poor attitudes begin to improve on their own

5. Poor performers and/or poor attitudes who are unwilling to change begin to leave the organization on their own

Ultimately, what this boils down to is two simple things:

Progress and Laughter.

ABC: Best Wellness and Peak Performance Program

> *"Happy employees make happy guests*
> *make happy accountants."*
> *-Kent Taylor, founder of Texas Roadhouse*

The "ABC: Best Wellness and Peak Performance Program" framework is an additional tool to help organizations build and perpetuate great cultures.

In my experience, the most effective and memorable "best place to work" initiatives fall under these three categories:

Altruism

Better Health and Fitness

Customized Coaching

Here's what each can look like:

1. "Altruism" through volunteerism, and/or the organizational mission has charity built into it.

2. "Better Health And Fitness" through offering unique fitness opportunities to members of the organization for free. Examples:

Boxing for fitness

Yoga

Brazilian Jiu-Jitsu

Group resistance training classes

Self-defense classes

3. "Customized Coaching". One-on-one sessions for team members available for free for those interested. Examples of what can be offered:

Goal achievement

Leadership development

Better time management

Reduced stress

Better relationships

Nutrition

Fitness

Meditation

Mental health

Summary:

If you're looking to create a unique wellness and peak performance program that will attract, develop, and keep the best talent in your market and field, the "ABC Program" will get you there. Here's a simple way to roll out your new Wellness Program and get it started:

1. Begin with one of the three categories. For example, "Customized Coaching".

2. Choose one of the initiatives from that category that you are the most excited and passionate about getting started. The one that will also have the most positive impact on your team member's success and happiness inside and outside of work. Example: Goals coaching.

3. Fully commit to offering goals coaching to your team members for a minimum of 90 days.

Don't overthink this.

Don't wait.

Just get started.

Making Your Guidance System Stick, and Common Cultural Engineering Pitfalls

> *"Advantages will come only to those who simplify for others. Making things clear and simple takes work. Being complicated and confusing is much easier."*
>
> *-Dan Sullivan*

The Three Keys to Make Your Guidance System Stick:

1. Simplicity (simple sticks, complex doesn't)

2. Repetition (over-communicate)

3. Conviction (believe in it 100%, hold everyone accountable starting with oneself)

The Three Biggest Things to Avoid When Engineering Your Culture (Common Pitfalls):

1. Long, complicated Guidance System (done is better than perfect, simple sticks—complex doesn't).

2. Under-communication of the new cultural Guidance System (team members and leadership must see and hear it daily for 90 days, then forever).

3. Not taking positive action on at least one important team member's suggestion within 72 hours of the anonymous survey completion.

> *"Repetition is vital. For example, let's say that you've told your employees that "customer focus is vital to the company's continued success". You have to repeat it in every conversation with employees, every speech, and every written statement. Bright people often think that if they've said it once, the point has been made. No, the point needs to be repeated."*
>
> *-Bill Conerly*

Summary

The most successful (and happiest) organizational cultures on the planet all have three simple fundamentals that create the foundation for world-class performance:

1. A Heroic Mission. The vision/mission is so big, bold, and inspiring that it pulls the whole team and organization towards it. *It is a clear aiming point for everyone.*

2. High Warmth. Team members are treated, and treat each other, with *care, respect, and dignity.*

3. High Standards. Standards of performance (and attitude) are much higher than other organizations in their market and field. *The best organizations have ELITE standards.*

How to Observe an Organization and Tell if it Has a Great Culture in Ten Seconds or Less:

1. Movement with purpose. Not frantic, stressed movement. Calm, deliberate, and continuous movement. The organization looks like a busy, productive beehive. High Standards.

2. Smiles and laughter. Customers and fellow team members are greeted with smiles. Laughter between teammates. High Warmth.

3. The newest team member knows the One-Sentence Mission Statement.

Here are three simple questions, that if asked on a regular basis, will build a best-in-class organization:

1. What's it gonna take to be the best?

2. Why would the best talent in our market and field want to work here?

3. What can destroy our culture (organization), and how do we avoid it?

We can break down each powerful question into what the answers may be for your organization.

1. What's it gonna take to be the best?

A heroic mission

High standards

High warmth

Relentless solution focus

Continuous improvement mindset

Sense of urgency

Best talent

Best leadership

2. Why would the best talent in our market and field want to work here?

Competent and caring leadership who they respect, admire, and can learn from

Surrounded by other great, talented, and caring teammates

An inspiring and energizing mission

Growth opportunities in knowledge (or position) within the organization

Fair compensation (within 10% above or below market average)

3. What can destroy our culture, and how do we avoid it?

Poor leadership/management

Negative and/or low-performing team members

No clear mission and direction

No clear standards of performance and driving core values

The following is the "World-Class Culture Architecture and Engineering" 90-Day Plan.

This seven-step process can be used by organizations of two team members all the way up to two million.

The seven steps are divided into three pillars:

1. Inversion. Figure out exactly what the biggest team member and leadership de-motivators are and address them quickly.

2. Guidance System. Create a guidance system of a clear mission and vision, core values, and standards. This guidance system should be so short that it can be written on a napkin, and so simple that it can be understood by a twelve-year-old. Short and simple is memorable and easy to implement. Long and complicated is forgettable and difficult to execute with consistency.

3. Success is in the Setup. This is talent acquisition and leadership development. The goal is to attract and keep the best talent in your market and industry through having the best leadership in your market and industry.

The seven steps:

Step One: Data, Data, Data

Step Two: Don't De-Motivate

Step Three: A Heroic Mission

Step Four: Highest Standards of Performance

Step Five: High Warmth (Core Values)

Step Six: Best Leadership

Step Seven: Best Talent

If you are looking for a quick fix for a culture that is struggling, here's the three-step process "minimum effective dosage" to get things back on track quickly.

Quick Fix #1: Team member anonymous surveys to see the true state of your organizational morale and happiness (and where specifically you can improve).

Quick Fix #2: Leadership each holds a meaningful, sincere, one-on-one conversation with one team member daily for three months.

Quick Fix #3: No more mindless negativity (complaining, venting, blaming, gossiping, and condemning as a communication style).

The "ABC: Best Wellness and Peak Performance Program" framework is an additional tool to help organizations build and perpetuate great cultures.

In my experience, the most effective and memorable "best place to work" initiatives fall under these three categories:

Altruism

Better Health and Fitness

Customized Coaching

Here's what each can look like.

1. "Altruism" through volunteerism, and/or the organizational mission has charity built into it.

2. "Better Health And Fitness" through offering unique fitness opportunities to members of the organization for free. Examples:

Boxing for fitness

Yoga

Brazilian Jiu-Jitsu

Group resistance training classes

Self-defense classes

3. "Customized Coaching". One-on-one sessions for team members available for free for those interested. Examples of what can be offered:

Goal achievement

Leadership development

Better time management

Reduced stress

Better relationships

Nutrition

Fitness

Meditation

Mental health

Making Your Guidance System Stick, and Common Cultural Engineering Pitfalls:

The Three Keys to Make Your Guidance System Stick:

1. Simplicity (simple sticks, complex doesn't)

2. Repetition (over-communicate)

3. Conviction (believe in it 100%, hold everyone accountable starting with oneself)

The Three Biggest Things to Avoid When Engineering Your Culture (Common Pitfalls):

1. Long, complicated Guidance System (done is better than perfect, simple sticks—complex doesn't).

2. Under-communication of the new cultural Guidance System (team members and leadership must see and hear it daily for 90 days, then forever).

3. Not taking positive action on at least one important team member's suggestion within 72 hours of the anonymous survey completion.

Six Great Books on Culture

> *"Learn as much as you can*
> *and help as much as you can."*
> -Dr. Marshall Goldsmith

1. Best-in-Class/Award-Winning

The Crystal Magnates by Truman Alexander

Awesomely Simple by John Spence

"Learn, learn, learn.
The greatest competitive advantage is knowledge."

-Mark Cuban

2. The Pursuit of Excellence

The Score Takes Care of Itself by Bill Walsh

The Culture Code by Daniel Coyle

"Genius is obsession in one area."

-Chris Eubank, Sr.

3. Service and Positive Impact on Others

The Go-Giver by Bob Burg

The 21 Irrefutable Laws of Leadership by John C. Maxwell

"We have a huge body of evidence, many, many studies looking at the frequency of giving behavior that exists in a team or an organization, and the more often people are helping and sharing their knowledge and providing mentoring, the better organizations do on every metric we can measure: Higher profits, customer satisfaction, employee retention. Even lower operating expenses."

-Dr. Adam Grant, author of "Give and Take"

Conclusion

1% Warrior Leaders take 100% Responsibility for everything that goes on in their family or organization.

You can observe your life through a mirror or through a window.

If you observe life through a window, you will look out into the world and find people or circumstances to blame, and excuses to make about why you did not succeed.

If you observe life through a mirror, you will look at that mirror and realize that you create and allow everything that happens to you.

Mistakes are inevitable as a leader. Admit your mistakes, take 100% responsibility, and move on.

No one expects you to be perfect.

In the long-term, you will be judged by the corrections you make thereafter, not by the mistake itself.

Lastly, when things go wrong, take 100% responsibility. When things go right, give all the credit to others.

> *"Beware of BCD: blame, complain, defend. BCD has never solved a problem, achieved a goal, or improved a relationship. Stop wasting your time and energy on something that will never help you. Ruthlessly eliminate BCD from your life."*
>
> *-Urban Meyer*

Taking Action = 97 Points

> *"To think confidently, act confidently."*
>
> *-David Schwartz*

On the scoreboard of "getting things done", knowledge is worth one point. Creating a plan is worth two points. Taking action is worth *97 points*.

Your 1% Warrior Leadership simple plan of action:

Maximize your energy.

Have one sincere, meaningful conversation with a team member every day.

Continuously upgrade your expertise.

Focus on the one Most Important Task for your one Most Important Goal.

Focus on your one Most Important Stop that is holding you back the most.

Find the one Most Important Person who can help you achieve your one Most Important Goal.

Master your time.

Ask powerful questions.

Prioritize attracting and keeping the best talent in your market and field.

Protect your culture.

That's your simple plan. It's worth two points. Taking action on it is worth 97 points. Nobody can do your pushups for you.

Win in Your Mind

I'll leave you with a three-step mental framework you can use to apply all of the mindsets and habits found within this book.

As long as you do these three things every day as a leader, you will never fail.

1. Be Useful.

> "Look after your people,
> and the business will take care of itself."
>
> -Brian Shel

Put your team member's, customer's, and community's happiness and success before yours. Who can I serve?

2. Flinch Forward.

"I am always happy when something is hard. Why? Because I know that most people aren't going to do what it takes."

Darren Hardy

Your success will be determined by the number of difficult things you do in a week:

Putting the extra hours in

Challenging others to be better

Protecting standards

Difficult conversations you have

Difficult decisions you make

Acting in spite of fear

Pushing your comfort zone and getting comfortable with discomfort

Taking risks

Etc.

What's the hard choice?

Do that.

3. 1% Warrior Mentality.

"If you're not getting better, you're getting worse."

-Joe Paterno

Get 1% better each day at the fundamentals and basics of leadership. Progress over perfection. Relentless solution focus. Continuous improvement mindset.

Leadership is the Answer

"People did not experience your intentions; they experience your behavior."

-Urban Meyer

The world needs more great leaders. Every problem in the world is a leadership problem.

Every solution is a leadership solution. Period.

Leadership is not a right or a burden. It's a privilege and an honor. Act accordingly.

Do everything you can every day to energize, reduce the stress, and be useful to your people.

And don't overthink this.

It's not that complicated.

Chapter Summaries

Don't overthink this.

It's not that complicated.

If you focus on the fundamentals found within this book, you can build yourself into a best-in-class leader in as little as six months.

Let's summarize the fundamental mindsets and habits of 1% Warrior Leadership.

1. The 12 Power Principles Of 1% Warrior Leadership

There are the 12 Power Principles of a 1% Warrior Leader:

1. Live by Example

2. Heroic Mission (Future Positive)

3. Ferocious Simplicity

4. Focus, Certainty, and Enthusiasm (Useful Charisma)

5. Energizer

6. Learn, Learn, Learn (Deep Domain Expertise)

7. Over-Communicator (Simplicity, Repetition, and Conviction)

8. High Warmth (Know, Care, and Believe in)

9. High Standards

10. Success is in the Setup

11. Listen, Shoot, Believe

12. Win

These principles can be applied to leadership in all disciplines:

Business management

Sports coaching

Parenting

Law enforcement commanders

And anyone in a position of leadership, anywhere, any time, any place.

2. Win the Day: The Leadership System That Never Fails

1. ENERGIZE and prioritize your #1 Performance Enhancer.

2. Have ONE Three-Minute Magic Conversation.

3. UPGRADE Your Expertise for 15 minutes.

Ask yourself at the end of the day if you did these three simple things.

If you did, it was a good day.

One Three-Minute Magic Conversation and "Upgrading Your Expertise" for 15 minutes are "minimum effective dosages". You WILL get positive results with little time invested. You can also increase your impact by having Magic Conversations with more than one person a day, or having a longer conversation with one individual. You can read and listen to educational materials for 60 minutes a day. The more time you spend per day on Magic Conversations and Upgrading Your Expertise, the better leader you will be. Period.

3. The Seven Challenges That Break (Or Make) Leaders

After 20 years of studying, practicing, and coaching leadership, the following "Seven Challenges" are the most common that leaders face:

The Seven Most Common Challenges:

1. "Mindless Negativity" in the organization.

2. Low-performing team members.

3. Attracting, hiring, and keeping high-performing team members.

4. Not hitting organizational and/or personal goals.

5. Not enough time in the day.

6. High levels of stress.

7. Creating more leaders.

Now that we know the "Seven Most Common Challenges", we can use the "17 Key Solutions" to give ourselves a simple and effective system to solve each challenge.

The 17 Key Solutions:

1. Lead by Example

2. Best People Setup

3. Three-Minute Magic Conversation

4. 5% Method to Law of Three

5. Don't De-motivate

6. Deep Data Diagnostics

7. No More Mindless Negativity

8. Positive Persuasion

9. Future Positive Focus

10. Say "NO" More Often

11. One MIG (Most Important Goal), One MIT (Most Important Task)

12. One MIS (Most Important Stop)

13. 1-2 Vital Functions + 1-2 Passionate Strengths

14. Minimum Effective Dosage

15. Upgrade Your Expertise

16. Maximize Your Energy

17. Feelings as Facts Listening

4. 21 Powerful Questions for Leaders

Out of the hundreds of questions I ask myself and the leaders I advise, the following 21 are the most powerful and effective.

They will help provide you with clarity of thought and the ability to know what the exact next right move is.

The solutions to all of your biggest challenges are already inside of you.

The questions:

1. Am I having fun?

2. What am I grateful for?

3. Is this thought helping me or hurting me?

4. What would the most confident version of myself do?

5. What would I do if I wasn't afraid?

6. What's the one thing?

7. What's the single hardest thing I can do?

8. How simple can I make this?

9. If I only had two hours a day to work, what would I do?

10. Is this getting me closer to my most important goal, or farther away?

11. Does this bring me happiness or growth?

12. What would the highest version of myself do?

13. What would I do if I was the best in the world?

14. What if everyone was just like me?

15. Who can I serve?

16. What am I doing differently than those around me?

17. What's it gonna take to be the best?

18. How can I achieve my ten-year goal in one year?

19. Knowing what I know now, would I do this or start this again?

20. If the challenge I am facing was happening to someone else, what advice would I give them?

21. What advice would I get from my 100-year-old self?

5. The Seven True Tests of a Leader

Over the years, I have identified seven tests that the best leaders consistently pass.

If you can pass these consistently, world-class results will inevitably follow.

Your people will be happier and more successful. What could be better than that?

They are so simple, you can start applying the mindsets and habits today.

Here are the straightforward "Seven Tests of the Best". I'll present them to you in the form of questions.

1. Do we win? Do I create positive change?

2. Do I energize others? Am I still a cheerleader, coach, and mentor even on the days that I don't feel up to it?

3. Do I create more leaders?

4. Do I take 100% responsibility for the organization?

5. Does my leadership attract (and keep) great people?

6. Do I stand up for my people?

7. Do I have difficult conversations on a regular basis?

6. 1% Warrior Goal Mastery

Here's the awesomely simple and effective 1% Warrior "Goal Mastery System":

Step 1: Set ONE 90-day MIG (Most Important Goal).

Step 2: Make a list of 10 to 20 activities that you can do to achieve that goal. Narrow it down to the ONE highest-impact activity, your One MIT (Most Important Task). Do this one thing every day for 90 days. If you miss a day, it's okay. Just don't miss two days in a row.

Step 3: Make a list of 10 to 20 things that you are doing that are holding you back from achieving your goal. It could be a habit or a limiting belief. Narrow it down to the ONE highest-impact thing to stop, your One MIS (Most Important Stop). Focus on that for the next 90 days.

Step 4: Find your MIP (Most Important Person) to help you achieve your goal. It could be a coach, mentor, model, trainer, therapist, etc. It could be an accountability partner who you will check in with and report to that you are sticking to your One MIT. This could be a friend, family member, co-worker, coach, mentor, therapist, etc.

That's all.

It works.

One goal.

One highest-impact activity to achieve that goal.

One habit to stop that is holding you back the most.

One person that can help you the most.

Don't overthink this.

It's not that complicated.

You got this.

7. Time Mastery: The Beat the Clock System

The "Beat the Clock" Seven-Step Time Mastery system encompasses the mindsets and habits of the people who get the most done on the planet:

1. Maximize Your Energy

"There are three keys to being fully charged each day: doing work that provides meaning to your life, having positive social interactions with others, and taking care of yourself so you have the energy you need to do the first two things."

-Tom Rath

In order to maximize your time, you must maximize your energy.

How to maximize your energy:

Eat foods that give you energy (that you also enjoy), and avoid foods that make you tired or give you "brain fog"

Get good quality sleep

Do exercise that you enjoy with people you like

Drink plenty of water

Spend time with energizing people

2. The Power of One (The 80/20 Principle)

> "Productivity can be boiled down to one word—FOCUS."
>
> -Mel Robbins

Have ONE key, measurable, non-negotiable, high-impact goal.

Do the ONE most important, highest-impact task every day to get you closer to achieving that goal.

Spend at least half of your workday on that ONE TASK that has the biggest impact on achieving your NUMBER ONE most important goal.

3. Say "NO" To Almost Everything

> "If you never did 75% of what you do every day,
> it wouldn't matter."
>
> -Dan Peña

Be incredibly lazy at the things that don't matter and incredibly disciplined at the things that do.

Practice "The Power of No". The happiest and most successful people say "NO" the most, and are continuously simplifying everything in their life and work.

4. Extreme Time-Blocking

"You will need to put up barriers to protect your time so you can serve more people."

-Russell Brunson

Extreme time-blocking is one of the ultimate secrets of productivity.

Forget "to-do lists". They are overwhelming and stressful.

Instead, schedule all of the important things you do into your daily calendar on your phone (or a physical daily planner if you prefer). Write out your day, scheduling all activities and time-blocking everything.

We must work from a calendar, not a to-do list.

5. Live Faster (Parkinson's Law)

"Success loves speed. Delay kills dreams."

-Craig Ballantyne

Having a healthy sense of urgency is one of the greatest competitive advantages in business (and life).

Focusing on being 10% more productive each day gives you over a FULL MONTH of extra productivity a year.

Parkinson's Law: "Work expands so as to fill the time available for its completion". The amount of time that one has to perform a task is the amount of time it will take to complete the task.

6. Work in Your 1-2 Strengths (Ikigai)

"Working on your weaknesses is a huge flaw. Get great at what you're good at. We only need to be good at one or two things and we can make an impact on the world."

-Dean Graziosi

Working in the areas of your one or two biggest strengths is one of the most useful productivity tools imaginable.

You will be happier and more successful when you work in the areas of your natural strengths. You'll get more done in less time because you are naturally good at it. You'll get more joy out of the work you do because you are naturally inclined to it.

7. Deep Learning (Leveraging Other People's Knowledge)

"Ignorant men raise questions that wise men answered a thousand years ago."

-Johann Wolfgang von Goethe

Leading = reading.

It is no coincidence that so many of the greatest leaders of all time read and studied on a regular (and extensive) basis. But reading isn't the only way to learn. Our knowledge and our mindset is a combination of the:

Books we read

People we spend time with and learn from

Audio we listen to (podcasts, audiobooks, music)

Videos we watch (documentaries, movies, YouTube, television)

Be very precise and ultra-careful about what you take into your mind and who you spend your time with. It shapes who you are.

Outstanding time mastery books

15 Secrets Successful People Know About Time Management by Kevin Kruse

The 150 Most Effective Ways to Boost Your Energy by Jonny Bowden

No B.S. Time Management by Dan Kennedy

One Thing by Gary Keller

Essentialism by Greg McKeown

Don't overthink this.

It's not that complicated.

Make it a habit to read for just 15 minutes a day.

You will never regret it.

> "Anyone who stops learning is old, whether twenty or eighty. Anyone who keeps learning stays young."
>
> -Henry Ford

Meeting Mastery

1. Brief. You can hold effective meetings for large organizations in as quick as 15 minutes. Only invite people who are necessary. Meetings of more than eight people have a "point of diminishing returns" in terms of productivity. Productivity fact: small teams working on a problem or innovation get more done. Jeff Bezos's "two pizza rule" at Amazon: Never have a meeting where two pizzas couldn't feed the entire group.

2. Bright. Positive and solution-oriented. Start and end the meeting on a positive note. This can be starting the meeting with what people did over the weekend, gratitude, positive things happening in the organization, positive performance by team members, and ending the meeting with clear action steps. If people absolutely need to vent or get things off of their chest, limit it to the first five to ten minutes of the meeting.

3. Future-focused. Ideas and solutions. No endless "archeological digs" into the past. Avoid talking about and complaining about past occurrences, past employees, etc. These things are now in the past. A great meeting is about today and the future.

4. Clear start times and end times. Start on time and end on time. Team members and leaders should not be late. Meetings should end on time. 10% of the time or less, the organization will be facing a challenge so large or pressing that you need to go over the allotted time. In my experience, most meetings should be an hour or less. 90 minutes maximum. As a leader, you will notice that you will begin to lose people's attention around the 55-minute mark, and anything over 90 minutes will be mentally (and sometimes emotionally) draining for your team. Brilliant advice from time management expert, Kevin Kruse: "Start meetings exactly on time and end them five minutes earlier than scheduled."

5. Clear agenda of five discussion items or less, starting the meeting with the <u>number one</u> most important topic of discussion.

6. The best meetings have strong "moderators" leading them, keeping everyone focused and moving. Parkinson's Law of Triviality: Most organizations and people will spend the most time on trivial issues and the least time on important issues. A strong moderator will cut off long-winded stories, tangents, and off-topic discussion.

7. Get closure on one topic before going to the next. If you can't make a decision on a topic or are becoming bored with the topic, either table it for the next meeting or make a decision now.

8. Avoid all cell phone or laptop usage unless it's absolutely to take notes or to look something up. No text messaging or answering calls; it's distracting and also inefficient because it's multitasking.

9. Clear action steps at the end of the meeting, with specific individuals who will do the work, and also clear deadlines. 3D Method: Make a Decision and stick to it. Delegate the task to someone. Set a Deadline.

10. Figure out your best meeting cadence for your organization. For example: Five-minute daily team huddles, 15-minute weekly meetings, 55-minute monthly meetings, 90-minute quarterly meetings, one-day yearly meetings.

Seven Steps to Delegation Mastery

1. If a team member or leader asks for the task, *give it to them.*

2. Allow people to fail safely.

3. Bring people problems, not solutions, and let them figure out their best way to solve it.

4. 10-80-10 Rule: give someone an objective/task and clearly define the process and result you are looking for (first 10%), allow them to work on the objective/task (middle 80%), then check the result and either approve or course-correct (final 10%).

5. Delegate things that people can do 80% as good as you so you can do the highest-impact work that you are strongest at.

6. Delegate as much as you can that is not your expertise. Spend 90% of your time (or more) doing the highest-impact work that you are strongest at.

7. Asking for help as a leader does not make you look weak or incompetent. When done the right way, it makes you look strong and smart. Help, and ask for help, religiously.

8. Talent Mastery: Success Is In The Setup

The best leaders attract, develop, and keep the best talent in their market and field. Period.

In any organization on the planet, 95% of your success is in "The Setup".

What is The Setup?

1. Create a big, energizing "Heroic Mission" that inspires and pulls the entire organization and its people towards it.

2. Do everything you can to attract, develop, and keep the best talent in your market and field who are deeply inspired and energized by your organization's specific Heroic Mission.

Don't overthink this.

It's not that complicated.

You are not just hiring. You are selecting true believers in your big energizing Heroic Mission.

Over the last 20 years, these are the three traits I have observed in the best team members in any organization:

1. High Warmth

2. High Standards

3. Energizer

Here's a simple breakdown of each.

1. High Warmth

Individuals with high warmth are lifters. They smile easily and they laugh often. They are quick to compliment or help a team member in need. They are warm and welcoming to new team members. *They prioritize giving over taking.*

2. High Standards

They are committed to excellence in everything they do—inside and outside of work. They are always looking to improve. They don't do the bare minimum, but continuously look to do "a little extra". They are self-motivated. Winners keep winning. *The best predictor of future performance is past performance.*

3. Energizer

They are enthusiastic and energized by the work and vision of the organization. This allows them to energize others, and also have the stamina to do the sometimes long and extra work required to get closer to achieving the big vision. They are confident and optimistic in themselves and others. They avoid being "mindlessly negative" and draining the energy of those around them. *They have a "fire and a spark" that lights up a room.*

In order to attract new team members with these three traits, you must ask yourself:

1. *Do I live these three traits as a leader?*

2. *Do our current team members in the organization live these traits?*

9. Culture Mastery: Cultural Architecture and Engineering

The most successful (and happiest) organizational cultures on the planet all have three simple fundamentals that create the foundation for world-class performance:

1. A Heroic Mission. The vision/mission is so big, bold, and inspiring that it pulls the whole team and organization towards it. *It is a clear aiming point for everyone.*

2. High Warmth. Team members are treated, and treat each other, with *care, respect, and dignity.*

3. High Standards. Standards of performance (and attitude) are much higher than other organizations in their market and field. *The best organizations have ELITE standards.*

How to Observe an Organization and Tell if it Has a Great Culture in Ten Seconds or Less:

1. Movement with purpose. Not frantic, stressed movement. Calm, deliberate, and continuous movement. The organization looks like a busy, productive beehive. High Standards.

2. Smiles and laughter. Customers and fellow team members are greeted with smiles. Laughter between teammates. High Warmth.

3. The newest team member knows the One-Sentence Mission Statement.

Here are three simple questions that, if asked on a regular basis, will build a best-in-class organization:

1. What's it gonna take to be the best?

2. Why would the best talent in our market and field want to work here?

3. What can destroy our culture (organization), and how do we avoid it?

We can break down each powerful question into what the answers may be for your organization.

1. What's it gonna take to be the best?

A heroic mission

High standards

High warmth

Relentless solution focus

Continuous improvement mindset

Sense of urgency

Best talent

Best leadership

2. Why would the best talent in our market and field want to work here?

Competent and caring leadership who they respect, admire, and can learn from

Surrounded by other great, talented, and caring teammates

An inspiring and energizing mission

Growth opportunities in knowledge (or position) within the organization

Fair compensation (within 10% above or below market average)

3. What can destroy our culture, and how do we avoid it?

Poor leadership/management

Negative and/or low-performing team members

No clear mission and direction

No clear standards of performance and driving core values

The following is the "World-Class Culture Architecture and Engineering" 90-Day Plan.

This seven-step process can be used by organizations of two team members all the way up to two million.

The seven steps are divided into three pillars:

1. Inversion. Figure out exactly what the biggest team member and leadership de-motivators are and address them quickly.

2. Guidance System. Create a guidance system of a clear mission and vision, core values, and standards. This guidance

system should be so short that it can be written on a napkin, and so simple that it can be understood by a twelve-year-old. Short and simple is memorable and easy to implement. Long and complicated is forgettable and difficult to execute with consistency.

3. Success is in the Setup. This is talent acquisition and leadership development. The goal is to attract and keep the best talent in your market and industry through having the best leadership in your market and industry.

The seven steps:

Step One: Data, Data, Data

Step Two: Don't De-Motivate

Step Three: A Heroic Mission

Step Four: Highest Standards of Performance

Step Five: High Warmth (Core Values)

Step Six: Best Leadership

Step Seven: Best Talent

If you are looking for a quick fix for a culture that is struggling, here's the three-step process "minimum effective dosage" to get things back on track quickly.

Quick Fix #1: Team member anonymous surveys to see the true state of your organizational morale and happiness (and where specifically you can improve).

Quick Fix #2: Leadership each holds a meaningful, sincere, one-on-one conversation with one team member daily for three months.

Quick Fix #3: No more mindless negativity (complaining, venting, blaming, gossiping, and condemning as a communication style).

The "ABC: Best Wellness and Peak Performance Program" framework is an additional tool to help organizations build and perpetuate great cultures.

In my experience, the most effective and memorable "best place to work" initiatives fall under these three categories:

Altruism

Better Health and Fitness

Customized Coaching

Here's what each can look like.

1. "Altruism" through volunteerism, and/or the organizational mission has charity built into it.

2. "Better Health And Fitness" through offering unique fitness opportunities to members of the organization for free. Examples:

Boxing for fitness

Yoga

Brazilian Jiu-Jitsu

Group resistance training classes

Self-defense classes

3. "Customized Coaching". One-on-one sessions for team members available for free for those interested. Examples of what can be offered:

Goal achievement

Leadership development

Better time management

Reduced stress

Better relationships

Nutrition

Fitness

Meditation

Mental health

Making Your Guidance System Stick, and Common Cultural Engineering Pitfalls:

The Three Keys to Make Your Guidance System Stick:

1. Simplicity (simple sticks, complex doesn't)

2. Repetition (over-communicate)

3. Conviction (believe in it 100%, hold everyone accountable starting with oneself)

The Three Biggest Things to Avoid When Engineering Your Culture (Common Pitfalls):

1. Long, complicated Guidance System (done is better than perfect, simple sticks—complex doesn't).

2. Under-communication of the new cultural Guidance System (team members and leadership must see and hear it daily for 90 days, then forever).

3. Not taking positive action on at least one important team member's suggestion within 72 hours of the anonymous survey completion.

Six Great Books on Culture

"Learn as much as you can and help as much as you can."

-Dr. Marshall Goldsmith

1. Best-in-Class/Award-Winning

The Crystal Magnates by Truman Alexander

Awesomely Simple by John Spence

"Learn, learn, learn.
The greatest competitive advantage is knowledge."

-Mark Cuban

2. The Pursuit of Excellence

The Score Takes Care of Itself by Bill Walsh

The Culture Code by Daniel Coyle

"Genius is obsession in one area."

-Chris Eubank, Sr.

3. Service and Positive Impact on Others

The Go-Giver by Bob Burg

The 21 Irrefutable Laws of Leadership by John C. Maxwell

"We have a huge body of evidence, many, many studies looking at the frequency of giving behavior that exists in a team or an organization, and the more often people are helping and sharing their knowledge and providing mentoring, the better organizations do on every metric we can measure: Higher profits, customer satisfaction, employee retention. Even lower operating expenses."

-Dr. Adam Grant, author of "Give and Take"

Book Recommendations

The Ultimate Leaders Library

The Success Principles 10th Anniversary edition by Jack Canfield

The 50th Law by Robert Greene

Tools of Titans by Tim Ferriss

The Charisma Myth by Olivia Fox Cabane

Talking the Winner's Way (How to Talk to Anyone) by Leil Lowndes

Essentialism by Greg McKeown

One Thing by Gary Keller

15 Secrets Successful People Know About Time Management by Kevin Kruse

The 150 Most Effective Ways to Boost Your Energy by Jonny Bowden

No B.S. Time Management by Dan Kennedy

The 21 Irrefutable Laws of Leadership by John C. Maxwell

Great Leaders Have No Rules by Kevin Kruse

Awesomely Simple by John Spence

The Score Takes Care of Itself by Bill Walsh

The Culture Code, Daniel Coyle

The Go-Giver by Bob Burg

The Crystal Magnates by Truman Alexander

Outstanding Time Mastery Books:

15 Secrets Successful People Know About Time Management by Kevin Kruse

The 150 Most Effective Ways to Boost Your Energy by Jonny Bowden

No B.S. Time Management by Dan Kennedy

One Thing by Gary Keller

Essentialism by Greg McKeown

Six Great Books On Culture

1. Best-in-Class/Award-Winning

The Crystal Magnates by Truman Alexander

Awesomely Simple by John Spence

2. The Pursuit of Excellence

The Score Takes Care of Itself by Bill Walsh

The Culture Code by Daniel Coyle

3. Service and Positive Impact on Others

The Go-Giver by Bob Burg

The 21 Irrefutable Laws of Leadership by John C. Maxwell

About the Author

A.J. Madden is a professional peak-performance coach and master transformation specialist based out of Bellefonte, Pennsylvania. He has a Bachelor of Arts degree in Philosophy from Bloomsburg University.

A.J. has spent the last 20 years studying and teaching the psychology and habits of high performance.

His clients are individuals and organizations that are in the top 1% of their field (or are trying to get there).

All of his clients are ACE's:

Astronomical goals

Clear integrity

Extremely committed

A.J. has coached organizations in 57 different categories in eight states and three countries. He has advised 34 female business owners and leaders. He has spent the last 20 years helping to build and improve businesses and organizations.

His mission is simple:

1. Help high-performance, high-impact individuals and organizations achieve their number-one most important goal and best share their special gifts with the world

2. To improve individual and organizational performance at any time, any place

3. To remove any obstacles and friction holding you back from unleashing your full and unlimited potential

4. To help people go from great to greater and get to the next level (because even the best can get better)

A.J. donates a portion of every client's fees to help feed underprivileged individuals and families.